D1082722

"Hurrah for the Ould Flag!"

The True Story of Captain Andrew Cowan
and the
First New York Independent Battery
at Gettysburg

by

R.L. Murray

Benedum Books
13205 Younglove Road
Wolcott, N.Y. 14590

ISBN

Paperback 0-9646261-3-6

Second Edition

Printed in the United States of America

For

Tammany,

my wonderful wife.

Table of Contents

Preface

Over the past three years, since the release of my first book, I have had the pleasure of speaking at dozens of historical societies and Civil War meetings. These opportunities have allowed me to meet hundreds of people with a passion for Civil War history – which is thrilling! Through this experience I have learned that there are a lot of people who are very interested in this period in our history.

Although the volume of interest does amaze me, what I find more incredible is the variety of interest. Readers range from the hard-core "buffs" that have hundreds of books and articles on the era, to a genealogist who is researching to find out more about a specific unit or battle because of an ancestor. I tried to keep this diversity in mind when I sat down to write, *"Hurrah for the Ould Flag!"*

The goal of my books is to present a historical record of New York units at Gettysburg, while at the same time giving the reader a better sense of what the individual participants went through. Rather than focusing on the broad scope and the massive movement of troops, I tried to focus on one unit, the 1st New York Independent, and then allow the participants to provide as much of the historical detail as possible. On nearly every page men such as Andrew Cowan, Henry Vaughn, George Brockway and "J.W.C." tell their interesting (and best of all, true) stories.

I would like to take this opportunity to thank you, the reader, for your interest and support, which allows me to continue my research. Thank you, and enjoy!

<u>Acknowledgments</u>

A special thank you to the following:

Tammany Murray – My supportive wife and great friend.
Ryan, Patrick, Rebekah and Katherine – (My children) for your love and support.
George W. Contant – A friend and author. Thanks for reading the manuscript and giving valuable suggestions and encouragement.
Dee Seadler – An awesome researcher at the National Archives.
David Hickey – Thanks for editing.
Kurt Kabelac – An excellent and unselfish researcher.
Sue Meyer – Thanks for writing suggestions and use of photographic materials.

Also: Nancy Assman, Connie Benowitz, Dale Bridson, Eric Campbell, Cindy Duprey, Cathy Gagnon, Anthony Gero, Scott Hartwig, Garth House and family, Malcolm Goodelle, Bill Grant, Peter Jones, Ed Kabelac, Helen Kirker, John Klink, Earl McElfresh, William V.P. Merritt, Christian F. Miller, Mary Nealon, Carl Peterson, Stephanie Przybyek, David Schultz, Ed Theimann and numerous others.

Special thanks to: Case Library at Colgate University, the Cayuga Historian's Office, the Cayuga Museum, the U.S. Military History Institute, the Filson Club, the Gettysburg Military Park Library, Kroch Library at Cornell, Aurora Civic Society along with the other historical societies and directors in Cayuga County.

Special mention of the late Mrs. Patricia House, who played a major role in the placement of a monument to the 1st New York Independent in Auburn, New York.

Chapter One

"God! I have never forgotten

the horror of that occasion."

When Andrew Cowan boarded a train bound for his home-town of Auburn, New York, in mid April of 1861, he was not sure what the future held for him. The nineteen-year-old Madison College freshman originally planned the trip in response to a plea from his former employer at the railroad office – the telegraph operator was ill and Cowan received an enticing offer to fill his former position for a month. This, however, was before President Lincoln issued his call for 75,000 volunteers to fight against the Southern states that were in rebellion.[1]

---

[1] Letter from Andrew Cowan to Reverend William H. Spencer, January 3, 1910. Part of the Andrew Cowan collection in the Special Collections of Case Library at Colgate University. Cited hereinafter as Cowan to Spencer; Letter from Andrew Cowan to James Tanner. Part of the Andrew Cowan collection in the Special Collections of the Case Library at Colgate University. Cited hereinafter as Cowan to Tanner. Cowan was offered $200 for a month's work – approximately five to ten times the normal wages for the same period.

The sense of adventure associated with the inevitable war to come seemed too much for young Cowan to resist. He heard that a group of volunteers were forming in Auburn, and "intended to enlist in Capt. Baker's Company" when he got home. Like most of his contemporaries, Cowan believed the war would be over in sixty days, allowing him to "be back at Hamilton & ready to be [re-] admitted to the Freshman Class that Fall."[2]

When Cowan's train arrived in Auburn, the six-foot tall lad grabbed his few belongings and headed for his parents' house.[3] Along the way Cowan exchanged greetings with many familiar faces including a neighbor, Terrance Kennedy. The "Captain," a title he received as the commander of the local artillery militia unit which fired the cannon each Fourth of July, quickly inquired as to Cowan's plans for the future. The details of the conversation are unclear, but the result was a commitment from Cowan to enlist in the company of volunteers being raised by Kennedy.[4]

On April 16, 1861, Andrew Cowan enlisted in the army, becoming the first Madison College student to volunteer during the Civil War.[5] Kennedy's unit eventually became Company B, of the 19th New York State Volunteers, an infantry regiment. Originally hoping his unit would serve as an artillery command, the "Captain" reluctantly accepted the infantry status after learning the war department "believed that the war would be over in sixty days, which would not allow the drill needed to make artillery soldiers of any use." Thus Kennedy's disappointed recruits received

---

[2] Cowan to Tanner; Cowan to Spencer. Madison College is now Colgate University, and is located in Hamilton, New York. The specifics of "Capt.Baker" or the unit's identity are unknown.

[3] Military Records from the National Archives in Washington, D.C. (With brown eyes and brown hair.)

[4] Cowan to Tanner; Cowan to Spencer.

[5] Kent Masterson Brown, "'Double Canister at Ten Yards:' Captain Andrew Cowan at Gettysburg" in *The Filson Club Quarterly*, Vol. 59, No. 3, July 1985. Cited hereinafter as Brown, "Double Canister;" Cowan to Spencer.

antiquated smoothbore muskets rather than fieldpieces and artillery implements.[6]

The next several weeks were ones of great excitement for Andrew Cowan and the other volunteers. They traveled to the nation's capital to begin their training along side units from other northern states. Upon arriving in Washington, the 19th New York set up camp and began drilling under the watchful eyes of cadets from West Point.[7] The men were convinced that one grand battle would decide the war, and the sense of adventure created by the anticipation of this event inspired the troops to work hard. The recruits marched, paraded, and drilled until July of 1861, when President Lincoln directed Brigadier General Irwin McDowell to lead his army into the field and meet the Confederates in battle.

General McDowell's plan called for the army to be divided in two: Brigadier General Robert Patterson assumed command of one force (18,000 men including the 19th New York), while McDowell personally led the other. Patterson's assignment was to occupy Brigadier General Joseph E. Johnston's Confederate troops in the Shenandoah Valley, thus preventing Johnston from reinforcing Brigadier General Pierre G. T. Beauregard's army – the force which McDowell expected to confront as he moved south.

McDowell's 30,000 troops slowly marched toward Centerville, taking two and a half days to cover a distance of just over twenty miles. Upon learning of this advance, the Confederates began shifting additional troops to face the Federal threat. Unfortunately for McDowell, General Patterson showed little aggressiveness in his front, allowing General Johnston's force in the Shenandoah to move in support of Beauregard. These reinforcements helped swing the tide of battle at Bull Run in the Confederate's favor, and potential victory for the Federals quickly turned into a disastrous defeat.

---

[6] Cowan to Tanner. Andrew Cowan became an Orderly Sergeant in Company B. "Our rifles were Harper's Ferry, Smooth Bore, Muskets, changed from flint lock and carrying an ounce ball and three buckshot."

[7] Cowan to Tanner.

The men of the 19th New York, along with most of Patterson's command, were not engaged in the battle – they were still several miles from the field when the fighting ended. After the day's action these units joined McDowell's disorganized mass of troops returning to the capital. With the sense of adventure having been replaced by the reality of defeat, most of the men in the 19th looked forward to the expiration of their enlistment.

On the morning of August 23, just over three months after officially mustering in, the 19th New York assembled on the parade grounds for what they assumed would be the final time. While shuffling into position, they noticed an artillery battery unlimbering at the edge of the field – its crew taking their posts beside the guns. Then two squads of United States cavalry rode up and halted on either side of the field. The New Yorkers' suspicions further intensified as a regiment of Pennsylvania volunteers formed a line behind them. Years later Andrew Cowan described the events which then transpired.

> **Then, as we stood in the ranks, the adjutant, Henry Stone, read an order of the Governor of the State of New York, turning the 19th N.Y. Reg[imen]t over to the service of the [Federal] Government for the unexpired term of its enlistment as a Militia N.Y. Reg[imen]t, which was two years...Then followed the reading of the order from General [Nathaniel] Banks to the effect that any one who should refuse to obey the order...would be sent to [do hard labor], until his term of two years expired - God! I have never forgotten the horror of that occasion.[8]**

---

[8] Cowan to Tanner. The 19th New York State volunteers officially mustered in at Elmira, New York, on May 17, 1861 (nearly a month after Cowan joined Kennedy's company). Frederick Phisterer, *New York in the War of the Rebellion,* 1861 - 1865 (Albany: 1912), 1956. Cited hereinafter as Phisterer.

Several other regiments from New York shared the same experience. Some of the units, including the 19th, were under the impression that ninety-day recruits would be released at the end of their term. Other units understood that they had enlisted in the New York State Militia for two years, but believed that after the initial ninety days of service expired they would be returned for duty in New York State.[9] While mutinies were not uncommon, only one company of the 19th refused to comply with the order. The bulk of these men quickly changed their minds after spending a day and night on the parade ground without shelter (only three men ultimately refused to accept the new terms of enlistment).[10]

Soon after this incident, Captain Kennedy was assigned the task of returning to Auburn to recruit additional men for the 19th New York. The captain persuaded the unit's commander that Cowan should accompany him, and the two set out on their mission.

Kennedy and Cowan initially traveled to Washington to make arrangements for their journey back to New York. Upon arriving at the capital Kennedy arranged a meeting with Secretary of State William Seward, also from Auburn. The captain took the opportunity to persuade the very influential Seward into supporting a plan for raising an artillery battery in Cayuga County. Seward liked the idea, and Kennedy emerged from the meeting with the Secretary's backing.[11]

As soon as Kennedy and Cowan arrived back home, the two began the task of organizing recruiting efforts for both the 19th New York and the new battery (although it was no secret as to which of the units received the greater emphasis). Cowan described the situation.

---

[9] Allan Nevins, *The War for the Union: The Improvised War*, 1861 - 1862 (New York, 1959), 176 - 177. "…mutinies developed in four regiments, and were not suppressed without great vexation." Governor Edwin Morgan of New York was under pressure from the War Department to meet the state's quota for recruits. New York had the largest quota and raised the most men, 120,000 in 1861 alone.

[10] Cowan to Tanner.

[11] Cowan to Spencer; Cowan to Tanner.

> We went to work recruiting for the
> reg[imen]t but we kept the biggest recruits for
> the battery. Assisted by the prominent men,
> we visited all parts of Cayuga County, holding
> meetings in churches and town halls, and ap-
> pealed for volunteers. It was what was called
> a "Whirl Wind Campaign."[12]

The new artillery recruits quickly signed on and began moving into camp. Without field pieces or the implements necessary
for instruction, Kennedy and Cowan were forced to improvise in
training. They decided to use infantry drills as a means of initiat-
ing the fresh volunteers into army life. The men marched and paraded nearly seven hours a day, walking over twenty miles rou-
tinely.[13] Finally by end of November 1861, with a full complement
of 156 men, the new battery was ready to head south.[14]

On the evening of December 2nd, the men boarded a train for
the first leg of their journey. After riding on the noisy bumpy cars
all night, they awoke in Albany. The stay in the state capital was
brief and unpleasant, as the following excerpt attests.

> Of our fare in Albany, the less said the bet-
> ter. If eating slops, and that in a hogpen, can
> be called living, then we lived while in Al-
> bany.[15]

From Albany they boarded the steamer, *New World*, and
headed down the Hudson River to New York City. Arriving on the

---

[12] Cowan to Tanner. Ironically, the 19th New York soon became the
3rd New York Light Artillery Regiment. An effort was made by this unit
to absorb the battery which Kennedy and Cowan formed, but their efforts were unsuccessful.

[13] Henry D. Vaughn letter. Part of the Vaughn collection at the Cayuga
Historian's Office. Cited hereinafter as Vaughn letters.

[14] Phisterer, 1559.

[15] A letter from an unidentified member of the battery which was
printed in the *Auburn Advertiser and Union,* 1/24/62. Cited hereinafter
as *Auburn A and U.*

morning of December 4th, the men again climbed into railroad cars and traveled all night to Philadelphia. From Philadelphia they went on to Baltimore, and by the morning of the 6th they reached the nation's capital.[16]

The men were only a small part of the thousands of new recruits arriving in the city. Arrangements were quickly made for the New Yorkers at Camp Berry, located "a little more than 1/2 of a mile east of the Capital Dome."[17] The camp appeared to be suitable to the men, and many quickly penned letters home telling their families of the events. One such letter was reprinted in the local Auburn paper so the community could be informed as to their movements. The following is an excerpt from this correspondence.

> **Our company has been favored from the first to the last since the day we arrived here. We were fortunate in being ordered to so good a camp ground for proper instruction in drill. We were fortunate in our reception by Secretary Seward, President Lincoln and others of his Cabinet.[18]**

Secretary of State William Seward seemed to take special interest in the men from his hometown. Mr. Seward and his family even visited their camp on Christmas Day. Over the next several years the volunteers from this battery would do much to make him proud.

---

[16] Vaughn letters.

[17] *Ibid.*

[18] *Auburn A and U*, 1/18/62. Letter signed, "A Soldier."

Chapter Two

"Boys, they shoot like they know we are here."

A feeling of exhilaration swept through the camp when the men of the 1st New York Independent Battery learned they were about to be issued field pieces. The Cayuga County men excitedly harnessed their horses on January 13, 1862, and awaited orders directing them to one of the nearby arsenals. The unit was originally issued two twelve pound brass pieces, but disappointment soon followed when they failed to receive a full complement of six guns. In a letter home, Sergeant Henry Vaughn described the events.

> Capt[ain] issued orders to have every horse saddled and harnessed, to go after the guns, Eve[ning] 7[:30] o'clock. We have just got back with our new cannon, all of them are wrought iron rifles, weight of barrel 850 lbs....We got

our guns from the Navy yard. I must say I
never saw so many guns in my life before.[1]

The cannon that the battery received were known as 3-inch
ordnance rifles. The black tubes were just over six feet long and
mounted on wooden carriages. The gently twisting grooves inside
the barrel caused the projectiles to spiral in flight, allowing the
rifled pieces to fire farther and more accurately than smoothbore
cannon. The 3-inch ordnance rifles quickly gained a good reputation among the artillerymen on both sides. They were light, accurate and sturdy – "Not one 3-inch ordnance rifle burst during the
Civil War..."[2]

Upon receiving the six new cannon, the unit began to look
and feel like a real battery. The men excitedly renewed their drill
and training. Their enthusiasm soon waned, however, when the
anticipated ammunition failed to arrive. Incredibly they would
have to wait another two months before finally receiving live
rounds.

Artillery tactics during the nineteenth century required a crew
of eight to service each field piece.[3] Every man had a specific task,
and the efficiency of each, as well as the teamwork of the gun
crew, determined how well the battery would perform. The
thought of combat inspired the men to work hard at mastering
their assigned duties.

Before the men saw any combat, however, they faced an enemy that proved to be far more dangerous than the Confederates;
this enemy was disease. While in camp many of the men became
seriously ill, and several died. The lines from the following letter
reveal the seriousness of the situation.

---

[1]Vaughn letters. The battery returned the smoothbore pieces and was
issued six rifled cannon.
[2]James C. Hazlett, Edwin Olmstead, and M. Hume Parks, *Field Artillery
Weapons of the Civil War* (University of Delaware Press, 1983); Warren
Ripley, *Artillery and Ammunition of the Civil War* (Promontory Press,
1970). These rifled pieces could accurately fire ten-pound projectiles
at up to a mile.
[3]Jack Coggins, *Arms and Equipment of the Civil War* (Garden City, New
York, 1962) 70.

Dear Sister,

> ...We have been unfortunate enough to lose 4 men since we came here, they were more healthy than myself when we started from Auburn, but they caught the measles and then Typhoid fever when low in strength and quickly died.[4]

The remarkable number of deaths in so short a time drew the attention of the medical authorities. An investigation was launched to see if unsanitary conditions in the camp were the cause of the sicknesses. The commission concluded that the problem had more to do with pre-existing conditions in the men than with the cleanliness of the camp. They attributed the high rate of illness and moralities on "the remarkable number of grown men gathered together that had never had the measles."[5] While this may sound simplistic and primitive, it was extremely accurate.

Sickness and disease were far more dangerous than bullets and shells to the Civil War soldier (for every combat death during the war, at least two men died from disease); this was especially true of the soldiers from rural areas.[6] The men from the farming communities were more susceptible to most diseases than their comrades from the cities. Because of the relative sparseness of the population in the country, fewer people were exposed to common childhood diseases, and thus did not have the opportunity to develop natural immunities.[7] During the war approximately thirty-seven men from the battery died from sickness and disease (twenty died in combat).[8]

---

[4]Vaughn letters.

[5] *Ibid.*

[6]Bell Irvin Wiley, *The Life of Billy Yank* (L.S.U. Press, 1952), 124. "In the Federal forces four persons died of sickness for every one killed in battle..."

[7]James McPherson, *Battle Cry of Freedom: The Civil War Era* (Oxford University Press, 1989), 485 and 487.

[8] Phisterer, 1560; Henry Vaughn wrote in December of 1862, "Death and disease are committing sad ravages in the army...Now twenty-five of our original men have paid the 'debt of nature,' – that is as much as

The men quietly went on with their duties, trying not to think about the unfortunate fate of their comrades. Further adding to the men's disillusionment, however, was the appearance of a disabled veteran from the Mexican War. The man was missing both hands, lost when an artillery shell exploded near him. Visiting the local camps asking for donations, he hoped to gather enough money to purchase artificial hands.[9]

In the middle of February the unit received orders directing them to a new camp. The change of scenery was just what the men needed; the prospect of leaving the unhealthy environment behind improved their morale. The move also created a sense of excitement as it was accompanied by rumors of possible action in battle. The following letter excerpt attests to the good feelings created by the change of camp.

> **...the day was beautiful, and as we marched up along Pennsylvania Avenue, past the President's house and past Gen. Barry's Headquarters in review, we felt sure of our mission, and that we had not mistaken our calling, in answer to duty, in our country's need...[and] we may be pardoned if we say, we were proud of our Battery.**[10]

Camp Griffin, in Fairfax County, Virginia, became the new "home" for the battery. The teams of horses pulled the limbers and cannon into camp at 3:00 o'clock in the afternoon on February 12th. Soon after arriving at Camp Griffin the 1st New York Independent Battery received live ammunition, allowing them to fire their pieces for the first time.

The battery was assigned to Brigadier General William "Baldy" Smith's division. As part of the artillery assigned to Gen-

---

to say, one man out of every six, has died, since we left Auburn. Awful."

[9] Vaughn letters.

[10]*Auburn A and U,* February 18, 1862. Signed "A SOLDIER".

eral Smith, the unit came under the direct supervision of the divisional chief of artillery, Captain Romeyn B. Ayres. Ayres, a graduate of West Point and a veteran of the war with Mexico, was a capable officer who patiently began training the volunteer artillerymen. His expertise and hard work during this period greatly benefited the batteries under his direction.

In the following weeks the men improved their skills. Excitement grew as rumors spread that Major General George McClellan's Army of the Potomac would soon be on the move. The entire army anxiously awaited the opportunity to strike a decisive blow against the Confederacy, which they believed would bring the war to a speedy and favorable conclusion.

The two armies had faced each other in northern Virginia for months, and the population in the North was becoming increasingly impatient. President Lincoln gently inquired as to when his commanding general felt he might move against the enemy. McClellan told Lincoln he was uncomfortable with the prospect of attacking the Confederates in their present positions. He proposed a bold plan that required the army to move on Richmond from the east, rather than from the north. Lincoln reluctantly consented.

McClellan's operation called for the army to be transported by water down the Potomac to the Chesapeake Bay, where they would land at Fort Monroe in eastern Virginia. The general reasoned that from there the distance to Richmond would be closer, and the unexpected maneuver would force the Confederates into a less advantageous position for defense. On March 17th, 1862 the Army of the Potomac began to embark for Fort Monroe.[11]

The men of the 1st New York Independent Battery were ordered to Alexandria, Virginia, at which point they would load their horses and equipment on boats. The unit arrived in the city on March 22, tired and wet from marching in the rain. The artillerymen dismounted and waited in the streets for word as to when they could move to the wharves. Upon inquiring with those in charge of the operation, the officers learned the battery could not board the

---

[11]Vincent Esposito, ed. *The West Point Atlas of American Wars*, Vol. I (New York, 1959), 39. Cited hereinafter as *West Point Atlas*.

ships until morning. Fortunately a pleasant bit of news soon followed.

> **We found we could not possibly ship before morning so the prospect was we should camp in the street the rest of the night, it being then about 9:00 but as good luck would have it, after we had unharnessed, the Mayor gave Capt leave to quarter his men in the Councilmen's assembly rooms. These were carpeted, warmed by coal stove, lighted by gas...They were the best quarters we have had since we left Auburn. Long live the Mayor of Alexandria!![12]**

The next morning, Sunday the 23rd of March, the men arrived at the docks.

> **We hitched up at 9:00 o'clock, drove down to the wharf & during six tedious hours managed to get our Battery aboard 3 different vessels, cannoneers & guns on a steamboat, put the horses on a schooner & the other part on another schooner. We walked the horses aboard a gang plank, & after our Battery was all loaded, the vessels that had us aboard were towed out into the stream and anchored.[13]**

The following day they began the thirty-six hour journey to Fort Monroe. Upon arriving, the ships remained at anchor for another twelve hours before finally being moved into position to unload.

---

[12] Vaughn letters.
[13] *Ibid.*

Once ashore and properly assembled, they marched four miles to the camp assigned to General Smith's division. Early the next morning Smith's command was on the move.

> **After leaving Fortress Monroe we proceeded very cautiously along the road to Newport News, and through other portions of the country occupied in part by rebel troops in pursuit of them. We had the satisfaction of opening our bright little cannons on a few rebels for the first time, about four miles from Newport News.[14]**

This action took place when General Smith ordered a section from the battery forward to fire at some Confederate cavalry scouts. Several days later the entire battery was again ordered forward, this time in support of some advancing infantry. The men, however, were instructed not to fire because of the presence of Union troops in their front. Soon the Southern gunners spotted the Federal cannon and began shelling their position. One rebel projectile hit a limber in Captain Charles Wheeler's Battery E, 1st New York Light Artillery. The limber exploded, but miraculously no one was injured.[15]

These first skirmishes were part of General McClellan's cautious advance toward Yorktown. By April 16, McClellan was ready to press the Confederates further. The Southern troops showed signs of constructing defenses on the opposite bank of the Warwick River, so General Smith was ordered to send a reconnaissance in force across near Dam No. 1.[16] As part of this effort Smith's chief of artillery, Captain Ayres, ordered up the four batteries under his command for support. These included, Battery F, 5th United States Light Artillery, Battery E, 1st New York Light

[14] *Auburn A and U*, April 29, 1862. Letter signed, "A SOLDIER".
[15] Vaughn letters.
[16] Stephen Sears, *To the Gates of Richmond: The Peninsula Campaign* (New York, 1992), 55.

Artillery, 3rd New York Independent Battery and four guns from the 1st New York Independent Artillery Battery.[17]

A member of the 1st Independent Battery from Auburn recorded the events.

> **...Our gallant little battery rode in on a gallop, took its position...[and] in a moment we were at work, forgetting all else save one thing – to mark our enemies. Thick and fast we sent our shells into the fort, now only about 650 yards off....Word was sent our captain that a charge would now be made by infantry on the fort, and that our little battery must cover them...For two hours we fought in this manner, during which time we were frequently cheered by troops around us, especially by the brave boys who had charged the fort.**[18]

Another member of the battery claimed they "dismounted [the Confederate's] guns and knocked down their flagstaff twice."[19] The Federal artillery fire raised havoc among the Southern ranks, one officer telling his men, "Break ranks and take care of yourselves, boys, for they shoot like they know we are here."[20]

Although initially successful, General Smith's force on the opposite side of the river failed to receive sufficient infantry support and was driven back with heavy losses. The Federal army continued its advance after the Confederates withdrew to York-

---

[17]*U.S. War Department. The War of the Rebellion: A Compilation of the Official Records of the Union and Confederate Armies,* (Washington,1880-1901), Series I, Vol. 11, Part I, 283 & 368. Cited hereinafter as *O.R.,* with all references being to Series I. The official reports filed by Ayres and Kennedy do not reveal why one of the 1st New York Independent's sections was not engaged.

[18] *Auburn A and U,* April 29, 1862. Letter signed, "A SOLDIER."

[19]Brown, "Double Canister". Mr. Brown quotes Private Edward Van Lear, from a letter is his personal collection.

[20]Sears, *To the Gates of Richmond,* 55.

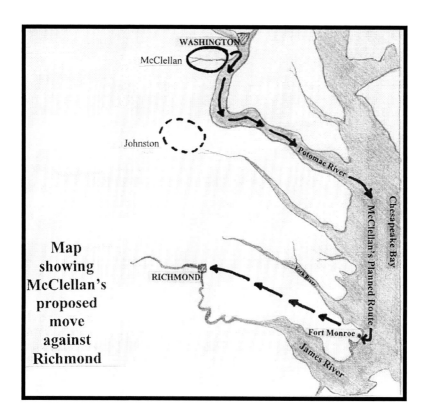

Map showing McClellan's proposed move against Richmond

Andrew Cowan
Born in Ayshire, Scotland on September 29, 1841
Cowan's family came to the United States
and settled in Auburn, New York, when
Cowan was a small boy.

United States Military History Institute
M.C.M.O.L.L. Collection

Secretary of State
William Seward
*Miller's Photographic History
of the Civil War*

Romeyn B. Ayres
Chief of Artillery for the
Sixth Corps and later a
brigadier general
New York at Gettysburg

A Federal arsenal in Washington. Location similar to where
the 1st New York Independent received their 3-inch rifles.

Miller's Photographic History of the Civil War

General Philip Kearney
A wealthy New York City
lawyer and a Mexican War
veteran.
*Miller's Photographic History
of the Civil War*

Henry Steele
First New York
Independent Battery

*Photograph from
Auora Civic Society*

An original photograph of Cowan's Battery crossing the dam over Warrick River

*Photograph from Miller's Photographic History
of the Civil War*

town. Upon his arrival at Yorktown, McClellan decided not to press the enemy, but rather to begin siege operations. For nearly a month the Army of the Potomac remained relatively inactive, until the Confederates finally evacuated their defenses on the night of May 3. Falling back to a position near Williamsburg, where the Southern troops received reinforcements and established a new defensive line.

During this period the 1st New York Independent Battery experienced a change in command – Captain Kennedy resigned. Kennedy accepted an offer of promotion and transferred to another battery, the 3rd New York Light Artillery. Although Cowan's promotion to captain did not become official for several weeks, he immediately assumed command of the battery.[21]

The Federal army continued their advance toward Williamsburg, where General McClellan ordered an offensive. Leading this operation was Major General "Fighting" Joe Hooker, whose troops quickly attacked, were repulsed, and were then in turn counterattacked. During the engagement Brigadier General Winfield Scott Hancock received permission to move against the Confederate flank. Assembling five regiments of infantry and Lieutenant Andrew Cowan's 1st New York Independent Artillery Battery, Hancock boldly advanced toward the rebel left.[22]

Cowan's battery of six guns fell in behind the second regiment as it marched out of camp. The prospect of such a move excited the troops, and their enthusiasm further intensified when they spotted an enemy redoubt after traveling only a few miles down

---

[21]Phisterer, 1561. Controversy surrounded this transfer. Apparently this was all part of an effort to absorb the 1st New York Independent into the ranks of the much larger 3rd New York Light Artillery Regiment. Cowan later wrote, "Kennedy had deceived us by letting us believe that he would never leave the Battery (he expected to take it along) but Capt. Ayres...,who was Chief of Artillery of our division...found out that Kennedy accepted the Major's commission and at once wrote to...[Brigadier] General William F. Barry, Chief of Art[iller]y" for the Army of the Potomac. The result of this letter was that the 1st Independent was to remain in Smith's division (and the Army of the Potomac), and that Cowan became its commander. Cowan to Tanner.

[22] *O.R.,* Vol. 11, Part One, 535.

the road. The column halted to deal with this threat. The redoubt lay on the opposite side of Cub Dam Creek, and two regiments moved forward to investigate. Cowan positioned his guns on a rise so as to provide cover fire if necessary.[23] The men advanced and discovered the redoubt to be unoccupied. Hancock left a small force in the earthen structure and resumed his march.

Pushing forward, Hancock found another abandoned redoubt, which he in turn occupied. From this new position the Federals could see other forts which the Confederates manned in strength. With this aggressive advance, Hancock's command became involved in the Battle of Williamsburg.

---

[23] *O.R.,* Vol. 11, Part 1, 532; L. Van Loan Naisawald, *Grape and Canister: The Story of the Field Artillery of the Army of the Potomac,* 1861 - 1865 (Oxford University Press, 1960), 55.

Chapter Three

"We Would Have Seen

Richmond Before Our Time"

General Winfield Scott Hancock's presence was a potential threat to the Southern forces around Fort Magruder. To this point, however, the Confederates were still too concerned with General Hooker to notice the small force on their left.

Hancock sent out skirmishers and ordered Cowan to unlimber his guns and open fire on the enemy forts.[1] The rain and mist that morning helped to conceal Hancock's position, but Cowan's shelling quickly revealed the threat to Longstreet. The general responded by ordering counterbattery fire, and later sent Major General D.H. Hill and his brigade commander, Brigadier General Jubal Early, to deal with the problem.

After firing twenty shells from his original position near the redoubt, Cowan advanced his guns 600 yards closer – increasing the effectiveness of their fire. Unlimbering on either side of a road

---

[1] Sears, *To the Gates of Richmond*, 78.

near a small farm house, Cowan's guns quickly resumed firing.[2] In the initial excitement, one of the battery's cannon became disabled through a mistake made by the Number Two man in the crew. Apparently he put the shell down the tube ahead of the powder. This rendered the piece temporarily unserviceable and it had to be taken to the rear.[3]

The remaining guns shelled the Southern targets, and in turn drew more counterbattery fire. One of these shots struck Private Edmund K. Terry, while in position at the front of his piece.[4] Terry, a young Irishman from Auburn who had only been married in the days before going off to war, was the first member of the battery killed in action.[5]

After Terry fell, Private William Sears grabbed the sponge and rammer, performing the duty of Number One the remainder of the day. The firing for Sears and the other men became increasingly difficult as the wet ground quickly turned to mud. The weight of the guns and the force of their recoil caused them to sink nearly to their hubs.[6] Even with these difficult conditions, the crews maintained a steady fire.

While the men of the 1st New York Independent dueled with the enemy, another battery arrived on the field. This unit, Battery E, 1st New York Light Artillery, contained four 3-inch rifles and was under the command of Captain Charles Wheeler. The lone battery was the only response to Hancock's previous requests for reinforcements – Captain Ayres instructed Wheeler to follow Hancock's aid to the field.[7]

Captain Wheeler's guns came into position on the right of Cowan's, near the farmhouse. His four cannon quickly unlimbered

---

[2]*O.R.,* Vol. 11, Part 1, 532.

[3]John M. Carroll, *Custer in the Civil War: His Unfinished Memoirs* (Presidio Press, 1977), 155; *O.R.,* Vol. 11, Part 1, 532 and 538. Cowan did not mention the incident in his official report, but he only referred to dispositions for five guns not six.

[4] *O.R.,* Vol. 11, Part 1, 532.

[5]*Auburn A and U*, May, 5, 1862.

[6]*O.R.,* Vol. 11, Part 1, 532 - 533.

[7]*Ibid.,* 528. The caissons were kept in the rear out of the direct line of fire.

and opened fire. Wheeler informed Cowan that he was to re-supply the 1st Independent's ammunition, if their chests were getting low. Cowan ordered two of his empty limbers back to Wheeler's caissons, exchanging them for full chests of ordnance.[8]

Unknown to the battery commanders, a serious threat was approaching. Generals Hill and Early were leading four regiments of infantry through the woods on the right of the batteries, hoping to flank the guns. Fortunately for the New Yorkers, part of these forces miscalculated the distance and emerged from the woods a quarter of a mile too soon. This regiment, the 24th Virginia, was led by Jubal Early. Seeing his mistake, the abrasive West Pointer ordered his old regiment to wheel around and face the batteries in preparation for a charge.[9]

After adjusting their formation, the Confederates began to advance. Watching this development, Cowan ordered his gunners to load with spherical case, and adjust the elevation of the barrels to meet the closer threat. The cannon soon erupted with flame and smoke. The gray and butternut troops bravely continued forward in the face of these exploding shells, closing to within 300 yards. At this point shouts rang out and the gunners changed ordnance to canister. These deadly rounds were tin cans packed with small cast iron balls. The discharge of these rounds tore large holes in the lines of the advancing infantry. Still the rebels pressed on, threatening to overrun the two batteries. General Hancock recognized the danger and ordered Cowan and Wheeler to retire. Withdrawing the pieces one at a time, each firing its final round and then limbering up and heading for the rear, the batteries were able to extricate all of their guns without a loss.[10]

Two men and a horse in one of Cowan's teams were wounded while racing back to the redoubt. Lieutenant William Wright's horse was also hit; it foamed blood but continued on,

---

[8] *O.R.*, Vol. 11, Part 1,, 530.

[9] Sears, *To the Gates of Richmond*, 79.

[10] *O.R.*, Vol. 11, Part 1, 530, 531, 533 and 538; Naisawald, *Grape and Canister*, 58.

carrying him safely off the field.[11] Wheeler's battery followed Cowan's – two of its pieces were delayed when they got hung up in a fence near the farm house.[12]

The two batteries soon unlimbered on either side of the redoubt. Because of the fast dash for the rear made by the guns, they came into position without having full crews – many of the men were left behind and ran back to meet the battery. The winded gunners soon gathered around their pieces and began positioning them in the muddy ground beside the fort.[13]

Pressing on after their initial success, the Confederates began to close on the redoubt. The Federal infantry fired several volleys into their ranks; the Confederates appeared undaunted. Suddenly an order was given to charge the oncoming gray lines, and three companies from the 33rd New York Volunteers led an attack which crashed into the rebels, effectively ending their assault.[14]

Soon after the battle at Williamsburg on May 5, the men of the 1st Independent Battery were on the march again. For the next fifteen days General McClellan slowly advanced up the Peninsula, closing on Richmond. As they approached, General Joseph E. Johnston prepared his defenses around the city.[15] By the end of May, McClellan advanced the army to within a few miles of the capital, where he again stalled.

General Johnston did not favor an inactive defense, and quickly seized the opportunity to strike at McClellan. The rebels attacked the Union left at what became know as the Battle of

---

[11] *O.R.,* Vol. 11, Part 1, 533; Naisawald, *Grape and Canister,* 58. The two men who were wounded were, Privates James Neville and Levi Cleveland (each only "slightly wounded").

[12] O.R., Vol. 11, Part 1, 530 – 531.

[13] *O.R.,* Vol. 11, Part 1, 539.

[14] *Ibid.,* 540; David W. Judd, *The Story of the Thirty-Third N.Y.S. Vol: Two Years Campaigning in Virginia and Maryland* (Rochester, New York, 1864), 88 - 90; George W. Contant, *Path of Blood: The True Story of the 33rd New York Volunteers* (Dover, Delaware, 1996), 128 - 139. Mr. Contant's fine scholarship gives an excellent account of this action. His primary sources strongly suggest that the three companies in the 33rd charged alone, and on their own initiative.

[15] *West Point Atlas,* Map 41.

Seven Pines (or Fair Oaks). The battle was indecisive, but during the fighting General Johnston received a wound which put him out of action; he was soon replaced by General Robert E. Lee.

Poor weather and McClellan's continued inactivity allowed General Lee time to strengthen his fortifications around Richmond. Lee, like Johnston, had no taste for a passive defensive. With his forces reorganized and the weather improving, Lee attacked. On June 26, 1862, the Confederates struck the Federal right at Mechanicsville. The following day, while the Federals pulled their lines back to a new position, Lee attacked again, this time near Gaines's Mills. These offensives unnerved McClellan, convincing him to change his base of operations to the James River.[16]

The change of base meant moving south from their line near the Chickahominy River, toward Malvern Hill. The troops viewed this action as a retreat, and became increasingly discouraged. Lee sensed another opportunity to strike.

On June 29, the Confederates attacked the Union troops at Savage Station. When this battle began, General William "Baldy" Smith's division was on the road south, headed for the narrow bridge crossing at White Oak Swamp Creek. Because of the threat to the Federal rear, Smith was ordered to countermarch and provide reinforcements if necessary. Cowan's battery, however, was sent on to White Oak Swamp.[17]

The bridge at White Oak Swamp was very important for the retreating Federals; if the Confederates destroyed it, the delay in crossing could cost the Union troops dearly. Cowan received orders to proceed to the bridge and place his guns in battery there. He was instructed to order the slow moving baggage wagons from his path, so as not to delay his movement. The captain rode just ahead of his battery "with revolver in hand to compel the Wagon drivers to give way enough to let us pass."[18]

The 1st New York Independent Artillery Battery arrived at the bridge and remained in position during the night and into the

---

[16] *West Point Atlas*, Map 46.

[17] Sears, *To the Gates of Richmond*, 272; Cowan to Spencer.

[18] Cowan to Spencer.

next morning – while the remainder of the army passed safely over the creek. Brigadier General William B. Franklin's Sixth Corps, to which Baldy Smith's division and Cowan's battery were assigned, then formed the rear guard of the army.

On the other side of the bridge General Thomas "Stonewall" Jackson opened fire with his artillery, but otherwise remained uncharacteristically idle.

General Lee's new plans called for a coordinated attack against the Federals. Unfortunately for Lee, his plans were not properly implemented and the only major effort was against the Union center near Glendale (or Charles City Crossroads). Here Major General A.P. Hill and General Longstreet's divisions struck Brigadier General George McCall's and Brigadier General Philip Kearny's Federal divisions.[19] The fighting was intense as the Confederates gained ground, but were thwarted with the arrival of Federal reinforcements. With daylight ending, the fighting eventually died down.

During the course of the battle, reinforcements, including those from Franklin's Sixth Corps, moved south to the crossroads to bolster the Union line. Late in the afternoon Cowan's battery received orders to proceed to the threatened area. As the limbers and caissons rolled down the Long Bridge Road toward the fighting, they encountered Major General Samuel P. Heintzelman, the commander of the Third Corps. Heintzelman instructed Cowan to report to General Kearny.[20]

Captain Cowan soon found Kearny's headquarters in the woods just off the road. The general did not believe there was room for him to deploy, but told Cowan to ride forward and assess the situation for himself. Upon seeing the field and its sufficient artillery, the captain rode back and reported to Kearny. The two officers agreed that it would be better to leave the battery on the road, and the general could send for them if needed.[21]

Cowan returned to his unit and instructed the men to get some rest, but to be prepared to move at a moment's notice. While giv-

---

[19] Sears, *To the Gates of Richmond*, 297.

[20] Cowan to Spencer.

[21] *Ibid.*

ing these orders an officer from an infantry regiment rode up and inquired as to the location of General Kearny's headquarters. Cowan offered to show him the way.

Captain Cowan led the officer to the general, but before he could turn to walk away Kearny asked Cowan to guide the officer's regiment into position – in the dark the general mistook the artilleryman for a staff officer. Complying with the general's wishes, he returned to the road and led the unit forward. After the regiment deployed, Cowan went back to inform Kearny as to the unit's location. Again supposing Cowan to be a staff officer, the general began giving the captain additional instructions. At this point Cowan spoke up.

"I beg pardon General," he said, "but I am the Captain of the Battery standing in the road."

"I beg your pardon Captain," Kearny replied, "return to your Battery and remain there until I send you orders."[22]

With this he returned to his guns and tried to get some rest. About 1 a.m., Cowan stirred as he noticed a few infantrymen passing. The captain, about to inquire some information from the men, heard, "Say, don't you know that the troops have withdrawn?"

Cowan jumped to his feet and exclaimed that no troops had passed by his position.

"Not on this road," replied the soldier, "but they have moved out by the same road to the right."

The soldier stated he was on the skirmish line and had only taken this road by mistake after becoming separated from his unit. Cowan suddenly realized that General Kearny must have forgotten about his battery when he ordered the troops to retire. The captain quietly woke the men and instructed them to prepare to move out. After riding down the road to confirm what the soldier had said was true, he ordered the battery to "left about," and with as little noise as possible they turned the limbers around in the road and headed back toward the Charles City crossroads.[23]

---

[22] Cowan to Spencer.
[23] *Ibid.;* Vaughn letters.

Arriving at the intersection, they found it choked with infantry on the move. Officers were prodding the men to press steadily on saying, "Hurry, hurry, boys, the Rebs may open on us at any moment."

While the artillerymen were standing in the dark waiting for an opening in the line, they heard someone say, "Leave me here boys, you cannot carry me farther." The voice came from an officer being carried in a blanket by four men. Cowan stepped forward and inquired as to the man's identity. The soldiers replied that the wounded officer was their colonel. Suggesting that if they thought the colonel could stand the pain of the bumpy ride, they could load him on a caisson. The wounded officer preferred the discomfort to the thought of capture, so they placed him on a caisson and the battery fell in line.[24] They marched the remainder of the night, and as the sun began to rise the battery neared Malvern Hill.

Climbing the slope the battery made it safely behind the defensive line, at which point they took the colonel to a makeshift hospital. With this done inquiries were made as to where the battery should be placed. They were instructed to park their guns in reserve near the Malvern House, and await further orders. No

---

[24] Cowan to Spencer. An interesting follow up to this story happened two years after the incident, in Washington, D.C. Captain Cowan was wounded in September of 1864, and was in the city recuperating. The captain's wife joined him there, and they often walked together. One day while they were strolling down Pennsylvania Avenue, Cowan noticed an officer in the Invalid Corps with a female companion. (Cowan continues the story)

> **As we drew near he eyed me closely, and I thought to myself, that chap is going to demand my pass, and I didn't have one that day – But just as we were about to meet face to face, he extended both hands, and then threw his arms around my neck, and said, Wife this is the man that saved my life and kept me from being taken prisoner. Blessed if he wasn't the Colonel who had ridden on the Caisson from X roads to Malvern Hill.**

Cowan stated that at the time of writing this letter he could not remember the man's name.

further orders came and the men watched the Battle of Malvern Hill from this position.

The narrow escape for the battery was something the men would long remember. Cowan's quick action had saved them from disaster. One member of the unit wrote home saying that if it was not for Cowan's cool leadership, "we would have seen Richmond before our time!"[25]

---

[25]Vaughn letters.

Chapter Four

"Now Captain,

let them have it!"

The battle at Malvern Hill was the last in a series of Confederate offensives launched against General McClellan's army during the Peninsular Campaign (the final week of engagements were collectively known as the Seven Days' Battles). Fortunately for the Federals, their defensive position for this final struggle was secure, and the rebel assaults were repulsed. Both sides suffered severely during the week of fighting: approximately 16,000 casualties for the Union and 20,000 for the Confederates.[1]

Soon after the Battle of Malvern Hill, Captain Cowan sat down and wrote a letter home describing the week. This letter reveals the stress that Cowan and his men experienced, portraying the true "glory" of war.

---

[1] *West Point Atlas*, Map 47.

Dear Mother:

> I am safe; my Battery is safe; had only two horses killed and one wounded; three died from exhaustion. Not a man hurt; had 4 or 5 taken prisoners since June 28th. I have been in four fights; have not slept but one hour out of the saddle, and have not eaten one meal in all that time; I am so weak and exhausted I can hardly stand.[2]

The major result of the Seven Days' Battles was that the Federal army retreated from its advantageous position near Richmond. Although the Army of the Potomac did not experience a significant tactical defeat on the field, the army's morale suffered greatly. The decision to retreat after every battle greatly discouraged the men – especially after their successful stand at Malvern Hill. Years later Andrew Cowan wrote a letter to a fellow veteran explaining the mood of the men during this period.

> The Army of the Potomac was demoralized. I never witnessed the like again. We had the right to stay at Malvern Hill [but instead we again retreated after the battle]...It was a great

---

[2] *Auburn A & U*, July 29, 1862. The men that Cowan referred to were those who had been sick and were in the hospitals behind the Federals lines. Unfortunately, the hospitals fell into Confederate hands when McClellan ordered a change of base to the south (on the James River). Later in the month Cowan wrote a letter to the Auburn paper hoping to find information about his missing men. *Auburn Advertiser and Union*, July 25th.

[Asking for information about] **George W. Crandall, Lewis C. Freeman, John Coughlin, William J. Miller, James Frain, and Peter H. Van Dyne. 1st 3 at the Trent House Hospital on June 28th; 2nd 3 at Liberty Hall Hospital, north side of the Chick**[ahominy] **River on June 26th and possibly escaped.**

blunder not to have held that field...[the men of the battery] **all agreed that it was a shame that we had been ordered to retreat.**[3]

Adding to the men's ill feelings during this period was the fact that the members of the battery had not been paid in months. An officer in Cowan's unit described the situation.

Uncle Sam seems to know what is good for us & keeps our money in his own pocket so that we can't spend it. He ain't bankrupt by any means, only a bit slow. It is now over 5 months since he favored us with the sight of money.[4]

Several factors contributed to the problem. First, the initial influx of hundreds of thousands of troops simply overwhelmed the payroll department. Never before in our nation's history had such a large army been assembled. The appropriations and paperwork necessary to pay this force took longer to organize than did the troops themselves. Once the bureaucratic efforts were under way, the payments could then be distributed to the troops.

The actual distribution of the payments was another problem. The paymasters often had to track individual units down in the field. These delays created backlogs for several months.

An additional problem plagued Cowan's battery. Another New York artillery unit tried to consolidate the 1st Independent into their ranks. The confusion created by this effort led to a temporary misidentification of the 1st New York Independent Light Artillery Battery, which further delayed the paymaster's efforts.

Finally, on July 23, nearly seven months after they were last paid, the men of Cowan's command received their monthly allotment. Most of the soldiers quickly made arrangements to send the

---

[3] Cowan to Spencer.
[4] Vaughn letters.

the money home to their families. With this problem finally recti-
fied, the men again turned their attentions back to the war effort.

In the weeks following the Seven Days' battles, the Union
forces under General George McClellan remained inactive –
which frustrated President Lincoln. The president was anxious for
action and shifted his hopes for victory to another officer, Major
General John Pope.

General Pope's earlier success in the West caught Lincoln's
eye. When the new Army of Virginia was created in late June of
1862, the president placed Pope in command. If nothing else, Pope
showed the aggressiveness that McClellan lacked.

In another major command decision, the president appointed
Major General Henry Halleck as general in chief – the top position
which McClellan held before going into the field during his Peninsular Campaign. The new general in chief and the president both
agreed that McClellan's forces should be moved from the Peninsula north to the Potomac, where they could support General Pope.
McClellan resisted this effort, but reluctantly began withdrawing
his forces at Halleck and Lincoln's insistence.[5]

The men of the 1st New York Independent Battery received
orders to march to the James River, where they were to load their
horses and equipment on ships. A member of the battery described
the events.

> **I halt to write and tell you that our Battery
> is here** [Hampton, Virginia] **right where we
> were March 26th 1862 and in good spirits ex-
> pecting to ship this PM – for we cannot guess
> where and now I must say that although we
> have had long & severe marches I am per-
> fectly well, & hope to meet the foe soon, again
> & Oh! that we may conquer.[6]**

After the horses, guns, and equipment were loaded on the
transports, the men settled in for their journey. The ships steamed

---

[5] *West Point Atlas*, Map 39 and 55.
[6] Vaughn letters.

down the James River and then turned north into the Chesapeake Bay. Unfortunately a storm blew into the area, tossing the ships in the rough seas and delaying their arrival. Finally on August 30th, the men disembarked at Alexandria, Virginia.[7] From here the battery marched toward Centerville, where the Sixth Corps was to concentrate.

General Pope's Union forces were engaged in battle with the Confederates at Second Bull Run on the same day that the 1st New York Independent Battery landed at Alexandria. The battle went badly for Pope; the Confederates fell on the Union left flank and the Federal army narrowly avoided a complete rout. The campaign was a major success for Lee and the Army of Northern Virginia, and another blow to Northern morale.

The victory at Second Bull Run provided an opportunity for the Southern army: with the Union troops disorganized from the defeat, General Lee could go on the offensive. Understanding that with limited manpower and resources the Confederacy could not win a purely defensive war, he felt it was important to take the war into the North. Hoping the invasion would further weaken the Union morale, and might even encourage Great Britain and France into recognizing the Confederacy, Lee guided his weary troops into Maryland.

On September 4, the gray and butternut troops began crossing the Potomac, and three days later were concentrated around Frederick, Maryland. Lee's presence caused a panic in the North. The seriousness of the situation demanded that the Federal forces be reorganized and made ready for battle as soon as possible. Under the circumstances there was only one man for the job – General George McClellan.

After the Battle of Second Bull Run the Union forces were concentrated around Washington. General McClellan moved quickly and efficiently to reorganize the Army of the Potomac, and advanced from the city's defensive perimeter on September 6.[8] Six days later the Union troops entered Frederick, Maryland,

---

[7] Vaughn letters.
[8] *West Point Atlas*, Map 65.

where General McClellan was handed a piece of paper which should have spelled disaster for General Lee's army.

A copy of Lee's "Special Order No. 191" was found, showing his dispositions and vulnerability. General McClellan wasted precious time before acting, however, giving Lee an opportunity to concentrate his forces at Sharpsburg, Maryland.

By the afternoon of September 16, major portions of the two opposing forces faced each other on opposite sides of Antietam Creek. Part of Lee's command, Major General A.P. Hill's division, was still at Harper's Ferry and would not join the Confederates at Sharpsburg until the following afternoon. General McClellan was also missing part of his command (although he substantially outnumbered the Confederates). Major General William B. Franklin's Sixth Corps (to which Cowan's battery was attached) was still moving toward Sharpsburg.

General Franklin and the Sixth Corps had previously been dispatched from the main body of the Army of the Potomac, with the assignment of moving against one of Lee's separated commands.[9] Franklin's troops moved west from Washington toward Crampton's Gap, in hopes of isolating and defeating Major General Lafayette McLaws' division.

As the Sixth Corps neared the strategic mountain pass, they noticed a line of gray troops blocking their advance. General Franklin deployed part of his forces and ordered them to drive the Confederates back. Cowan's six rifled pieces were sent forward, coming into battery in support of Brigadier General W.T.H. Brooks' brigade. The Federals pushed McLaws' troops back and then occupied the pass.[10] They remained there for two days, until Franklin received orders to proceed toward Antietam and rejoin the rest of the army.[11]

---

[9] *West Point Atlas*, Map 66; *O.R.*, Vol. 19, Part I, 374 - 375. He was also instructed to move toward Harper's Ferry, where over 10,000 Federals were surrounded and about to surrender. Unfortunately for the Union troops at Harper's Ferry, Franklin did not aggressively press forward and the garrison was captured.

[10] Milton A. Kinney's letter to his sister, letter dated Sept. 29th. Printed in the *Auburn A & U*; *O.R.*, Vol. 19, Part I, 375.

[11] *O.R.*, Vol. 19, Part I, 375.

Just after dawn on the morning of September 17th, Major General William Smith's division (along with Cowan's battery) marched out of camp toward Sharpsburg. The column neared the Federal lines around 10:00 a.m.[12] A member of the battery described their approach to the field.

> **Passing over ploughed fields, steep hills, and other ugly places, where the cannoneers had to put shoulders to the wheels to help the horses, we finally plunged down a hill, forded the Antietam; rising another hill, I found we were where the enemy's shell could reach us...[Then] plunging through a wood, we came quickly on a field where the trampled corn, scattered knapsacks, and here and there a dead body, told us that the battle had raged there earlier in the day.[13]**

Cowan's command, along with several other batteries, crossed the Antietam and headed to the northern end of the field, where the heaviest fighting had taken place earlier that morning. Major F.N. Clark, the chief of artillery for the Second Corps, led the guns into position. He placed the pieces on the crest of a hilly field just to the left (south) of the 49th Pennsylvania. Orders rang out and the guns were unlimbered. The gunners sighted the pieces and elevations were adjusted; their target was some artillery in the woods three-quarters of a mile away.[14]

As Cowan's gunners began loading and firing, they noticed Federal infantry in their front. Brigadier General Winfield Scott Hancock also saw the men, and rode forward to inquire why they were there. The troops were members of the 49th Pennsylvania. They informed Hancock that the officer in charge of their company, Major Hurling, placed them in position, but then made his

---

[12] "J.W.C." letter dated Sept. 27th, in *Auburn A & U; O.R.,* Vol. 19, Part I, 376.

[13] "J.W.C." letter dated Sept. 27th, *Auburn A and U.*

[14] *Ibid.; O.R.,* Vol. 19, Part I, 407. "J.W.C.'s" letter does not name the aid but General Hancock did in his official report.

way to the rear. Hancock sent for Hurling, and then severely cursed him out in front of his men. The general then ordered the unit to retire.[15]

As the last of the soldiers cleared the battery's front, Hancock rode over to speak with Captain Cowan. Removing a flask from his pocket, Hancock took a sip, slipped it back into his jacket, and calmly turned to Cowan saying, "Now, Captain, let them have it!"[16] With this Cowan's guns roared back into action.

For the next three hours the men of the 1st New York fired shells and solid shot at the enemy's artillery and infantry. Focusing their attention mainly on the Confederate batteries, the gunners occasionally fired on the infantry whenever the gray formations were sighted. Cowan's guns drew counterbattery fire, causing shells to fly over and through their position. The men calmly continued servicing their pieces while Captain Cowan rode back and forth on his horse, encouraging his crews.[17]

While holding a lead limber horse in one of the 1st Independent's teams, a soldier noticed an artillery shell crash into the ground in front of him. Fortunately the shell was fired from a rifled cannon, causing the spiraling projectile to corkscrew into the sod – exploding harmlessly under ground. Another crewman, Private John Lanning, was holding a lead limber horse in another team. Suddenly a shell struck the horse that he was holding, killing the animal. At first it was feared that Lanning was seriously injured because he was covered with spattered horse flesh and blood, but fortunately he was unharmed.[18]

Throughout the course of the battle the men of the battery witnessed some fierce fighting. A member of the unit wrote home describing a skirmish.

---

[15] John Michael Priest, *Antietam: The Soldier's Battle* (Oxford University Press, 1989), 173. Hurling's command was Company C, of the 49th Pennsylvania.

[16] Priest, *Antietam*, 185 - 186.

[17] "J.W.C." letter, *Auburn A and U.*

[18] *Ibid.*; Priest, *Antietam*, 294; *O.R.*, Vol. 19, Part 1, 405.

Brigadier General
Winfield Scott Hancock

*Miller's Photographic History
of the Civil War*

Confederate artillerymen killed at Antietam.
Cowan's gunners may have exchanged fire
with batteries in this area.

Miller's Photographic History of the Civil War

Captain Andrew Cowan

**Lieutenant Henry
Vaughn**
Aurora Civic Society

George Chidester
Aurora Civic Society

Enlisted men in the First New York Independent Battery

Charles H. Gaylord
Helen Kirker collection

Thomas Sherman
Aurora Civic Society

Ithiel Winters
Aurora Civic Society

John VanDeripe
Aurora Civic Society

**Brigadier General
Henry J. Hunt**
Commander of Artillery
Army of the Potomac

*Photograph courtesy Gettysburg
Military
Historical Park Library*

**Major General
John Sedgwick**

Sedgwick commanded the
Sixth Corps at Gettysburg
and was much beloved by
his men.
Andrew Cowan later named
his son
Gilbert Sedgwick Cowan
in honor of his former
commander.

*Photograph courtesy Gettysburg Military
Historical Park Library*

I saw something I never saw before, that was two columns of infantry stand up and fire at one another. There was no charging about it, but they marched up to within musket range of each other, loaded and fired at will. When one regiment was thinned out its place was supplied by another.[19]

The battery remained in position for the remainder of the 17th – with only brief counterbattery action flaring up again at 4:00 o'clock in the afternoon. The men welcomed the setting of the sun and the inactivity that accompanied it.

The following day the battery remained in position, watching the Confederates across the field. Neither side initiated any major activity, and that night Lee's army withdrew through town and across the Potomac River.

When the Federals awoke the next morning, they found the field unoccupied. Part of the Federal lines advanced over the ground which the Confederates had previously defended. The carnage they witnessed is documented in the following accounts from Cowan's men.

We found that [a] **battery** [we had previously exchanged fire with] **had left twelve dead horses, two limber chests blown up, a broken wheel with signs of at least one gun having been dismounted, while the ground around was ploughed with our shells; blood soaked the ground, where many bodies doubtless had lain.[20]**

I will not disgust you with details, except I have seen, for the first time a leg amputated; and...I came across their ambulance depot where the rebel wounded were cared for, and they had been in such haste to leave, that

---

[19] "Kinney" letter, *Auburn A and U.*

[20] "J.W.C." *letter, Auburn A and U.*

there were piles of fingers, hands, feet & limbs, yet unburied...[21]

I had read of the postures of the dead on a battle field. Here was everything I had either read, heard of, or imagined, forming one grand horrible picture...[22]

---

[21] Vaughn letters.

[22] 'J.W.C." *letter, Auburn A and U.*

Chapter Five

"Soon we shall hear

the earnest

booming of cannon."

The Battle of Antietam was the single bloodiest day in American history. For the men of the 1st New York Independent and the rest of the Army of the Potomac, however, there was a glimmer of encouragement amidst the horrible losses: the Confederates were forced to retreat.

Following the conflict at Sharpsburg, President Lincoln and General Halleck urged McClellan to move against Lee before he could replenish the Army of Northern Virginia's depleted ranks. They spent weeks prodding, but the general remained relatively inactive. Finally the president's patience ran out, and McClellan was permanently removed from command.

In early November, Major General Ambrose Burnside was selected to command the Army of the Potomac. Burnside's earlier effort in leading amphibious operations along the North Carolina coast was one of the few glimmers of hope in the Union war effort.[1] The president needed someone to command the army, and at the time Burnside seemed the logical choice. Although lacking confidence and charisma, at least he would be a man of action.

Ambrose Burnside soon formulated a plan of attack. He hoped to concentrate his forces at Warrenton, Virginia (so as to threaten Culpeper and Gordonsville). Then he wanted to quickly shift the army southeast, crossing the Rappahannock at Fredericksburg before the Confederates could move to block his advance.[2] Burnside reasoned that such a move would be advantageous for two reasons: it would provide the Federals with a safer line of communications for re-supply, and it would force Lee into a less favorable position for defense.

General Burnside began moving the army toward Fredericksburg on November 15, two days later the vanguard of his forces arrived across from the city. For the next week the general waited in frustration because the pontoons needed for bridge construction failed to arrive. In the mean time, Lee responded by sending Lieutenant General James Longstreet's Corps to establish a defensive line across the river from the Union army. Burnside's opportunity for an unopposed crossing was gone.

On December 10, Cowan's battery joined the row of Federal guns on Stafford Heights – an elevated position overlooking Fredericksburg. The location was strategically important because the Army of the Potomac's artillery could provide cover fire for the river crossing, or defensive fire in case the Union troops were counterattacked.

The following morning, the 11th, the engineers were in the process of constructing a bridge from the recently delivered pontoons. Progress was slowed by the presence of Confederate sharpshooters, who were picking off the men as they worked. Small arms fire did little to discourage the rebels, who took cover in the abandoned houses in Fredericksburg. To combat these snipers the Federal artillery was directed to fire into the city, but the shelling was only slightly effective. Finally several batteries, including

---

[1] *West Point Atlas,* 71.
[2] *Ibid.*

Cowan's, were ordered to move closer for more accurate support.[3]

Twelve teams of horses pulled the 1st New York Independent's limbers and caissons down the road leading from the heights. The battery quickly came into position beside the river, and opened fire on the houses. They continued shelling the remainder of the afternoon, battling both the Confederates and the harsh elements. The bitter cold took its toll on the men and cannon. Each discharge pounded the wooden wheels and carriages against the frozen ground, which eventually cracked the wooden axles on three of the guns.[4]

With three cannon out of action, and the bridge nearly complete, the battery was ordered back up the heights. As the teams hauled the battery back up the slope, the Federal troops were crossing the river in large numbers. Upon reaching the crest of the hill, Captain Cowan set out to find replacement parts so his crews could repair their broken axles. Making his way to Brigadier General Henry Hunt's headquarters, he informed the army's chief of artillery of his problem. General Hunt told Cowan that there were no axles available, and his unit would be out of commission until parts arrived from Washington. Refusing to accept this setback, Cowan and his men managed to make the repairs using materials they could scrape together. With their patched-up carriages, the battery reported for duty at 6:00 a.m. the following morning.[5]

The men of the 1st Independent spent the remainder of the battle providing cover fire from different locations on the heights. Across the river the Union infantry experienced one of their most devastating defeats of the war. Thousands of men fell in front of the wall on Marye's Heights. Burnside's army suffered over 12,000 casualties at Fredericksburg, while the Confederates lost less than half that many.

---

[3] *O.R.,* Vol. 21, Part I, 216; "J.W.C." letter, dated Jan. 3, 1863, *Auburn A and U.*

[4] *Ibid*

[5] *O.R.,* Vol. 21, Part I, 216.

After the battle the two armies remained in their positions across the river from each other. Burnside, though discouraged, was still determined to go on the offensive. In January he again tried a flanking movement to force Lee from his defensive positions. This effort ended in failure when the weather turned bad, making the roads impassable. The affair became known as the "Mud March," and did little to inspire the already demoralized troops. A member of the battery wrote home describing the fiasco.

> **The roads were in the worst possible condition; every few rods down would go the wheels to the hubs, and the cannoneers were obliged to aid in lifting the carriages out...[After the march the men were] exhausted by thirty-six hours of hard labor in cold, rain and mud, [and] threw themselves on the wet ground and slept.**[6]

In the weeks following the "Mud March," the men established winter quarters and prepared for the coming months of foul weather and inactivity. The lack of success against the Confederates weighed heavily on the Union soldiers. Constant defeats and high casualties caused the men to lose confidence in their leadership; to them the changes in command made little difference, defeat and loss of lives seemed inevitable.

The mood of the soldiers in the 1st Independent was further affected by another long period of no pay. The months without money were hard on the men, but more important, it was often devastating for their families back home – they depended on these funds to sustain them. The following is an excerpt from a letter which appeared in the local paper in Auburn in early February of 1863.

> **Much suffering has been caused by the delay in paying the troops, especially to the families at home who are dependent on that**

---

[6]"G.W.C." letter ("J.W.C."), dated Jan. 11, 1862, in *Auburn A & U.*

small sum to sustain life. I have seen strong men weep over the suffering of their wives and children at home. Even this morning a letter was shown to me by a man [whose]...**eldest son had died** [because of their lack of food].[7]

During the last week of January, 1863, the men finally received their pay. Additionally, the men heard the news concerning a change in command; General Burnside had been relieved and Major General Joseph Hooker was now in charge of the Army of the Potomac.

Gradually the spirits of the men rose as the enthusiasm and confidence demonstrated by "Fighting Joe" Hooker filtered down through the ranks. The general instituted some practical changes, which did much to raise the morale; food, living conditions in camps, and medical care all improved.

Weeks passed and the weather began to improve. The rising temperature signaled the beginning of a new season of campaigning. The men's letters during this period revealed they were anxious for action.

Soon we shall hear the earnest booming of cannon and the rattle of musketry. How my heart aches to have it commenced again upon this free land of ours.[8]

This statement shows that many of the men were actually looking forward to the start of a new campaign. Naturally they were in no hurry to see a battle for the battle's sake, but they hoped the next major clash would be the last. The men in the bat-

---

[7]*Auburn A and U,* Feb. 10, 1863. The letter stated that his children were "suffering from cold and hunger, and all the food in the house a few cold potatoes the children had received in charity..." Ironically, by the time this letter appeared in the local paper the men of the battery had already been paid.

[8] Vaughn letters.

tery desperately wanted to go home, but most were only willing to do so after the job of restoring the Union was complete.

Late in April of 1863, General Hooker set his troops in motion. "Fighting Joe" devised a good plan; he was going to try to outflank Lee and force him to give battle out in the open. Hooker sent three of his seven corps on a quick march north and then west from Fredericksburg. They crossed the Rappahannock River at Kelly's Ford, and surprised the Confederates there.

Part of Hooker's overall strategy called for Major General John Sedgwick's Sixth Corps, along with the First Corps, to re-cross the river below Fredericksburg in an effort to distract Lee. Hooker hoped to hold General Lee in position long enough for the major portion of the Army of the Potomac to slip off and around behind the Confederate's left flank. Once Lee discovered the ruse, Sedgwick was to advance directly west, thus trapping Lee between two Federal armies. Unfortunately for Sedgwick the details of these instructions were vague, and later miscommunication between himself and Hooker caused major problems.

On the last day of April, Cowan's battery, along with the other Sixth Corps units, moved out in a rainstorm. Slowly struggling along in the cold and mud, the battery arrived on Stafford Heights – the same position they had occupied the previous December.[9]

The next day, May 2, Cowan's six cannon followed the infantry as they moved toward the river. The teams pulled the limbers and cannon across the Rappahannock, where they deployed to provide cover fire for the advancing Union troops. The six guns quickly engaged the Southern cannon in counterbattery fire, and exchanged volleys with them for the remainder of the day.[10]

In the meantime, General Hooker's forces near Chancellorsville were heavily engaged, and the Union commander was about to falter. During the battle Hooker became inexplicably timid, and eventually surrendered the initiative to Lee. Never one to waste an opportunity to attack, General Lee boldly sent Lieutenant General Thomas "Stonewall" Jackson on a flanking maneuver around the

---

[9] "J.W.C." letter, dated May 6, 1863, *Auburn A and U.*

[10] *Ibid.*; *O.R.*, Vol. 25, Part I, 612.

Federal right. From here Jackson's troops launched their attack, crashing into the unsuspecting Eleventh Corps. Fortunately for Hooker and the Federals, darkness fell on the field before Jackson's tired troops could fully exploit their success.

That evening General Sedgwick received orders from Hooker – attack the Southern troops on the heights and drive them back. Hooker believed this would open the way for the Sixth Corps to advance and threaten Lee's rear.

The next day, May 3, Sedgwick ordered the corps to move north along the Old Richmond Road and occupy the city. Cowan's unit came into battery less than one-quarter of a mile from the outskirts of Fredericksburg, where they again engaged the Southern gunners in counterbattery fire.[11] Throughout the morning Sedgwick's subordinates made preparations for the attack. The thought of approaching the same heights that Burnside had been unable to overrun five months earlier was unnerving. Unlike the first battle of Fredericksburg, the Confederates were now in much smaller numbers and lacked the firepower to turn back the Federals.

The Sixth Corps infantry advanced and began their attack on Marye's Heights. To assist this effort, several batteries, including Cowan's, fired shells at the defenders. The 1st Independent's guns focused on the earthen forts, which the Southern troops had previously constructed to protect their artillery. From these fortified positions the gray clad cannoneers fired into the massed ranks of Federal infantry.[12] One of Cowan's gunners penned a note home during the fighting.

> **The 2nd Battle of Fredericksburg is now raging with a desperation only exceeded by the First... Hooker is with the main part of the Army rapidly going to the rear of the enemy. His distant cannonading can distinctly be heard. I am so excited with the roar of cannon and musketry that I can hardly write. The**

---

[11] *O.R.,* Vol. 25, Part I, 612.
[12] "J.W.C." letter, *Auburn A and U*; Naisawald, *Grape and Canister*, 319.

> crash of bursting shells as they hurl them
> against our brave boys is awful.[13]

After three unsuccessful efforts, the Federals finally overran
the heights. Another member of the battery documented these
events.

> We had a fine view of them [the Federal infan-
> try] as they charged over the works and drove
> the enemy out. Our division gave one cheer
> for them, and rushed forward... on they went,
> our Batteries firing as fast as they could load,
> over their heads, and bursting shell in every
> part, till they too had taken the rifle pits and
> driven the enemy from the forts...[14]

During the attack Corporal William Dempsey carefully straddled the stock of the third gun, and sighted the piece. After the
necessary adjustments were made he stepped back and called,
"Ready!" The powder cartridge was pricked open, primer inserted,
and the lanyard hooked to the primer. Dempsey then yelled,
"Fire!" The shell hurled out of the muzzle and sailed directly into
one of the forts, exploding a limber chest. This type of accurate
firing brought praise from many of the surrounding units.[15]

By 1:00 o'clock in the afternoon the Federals occupied
Marye's Heights. Cowan ordered his guns to be limbered and five
of the battery's cannon headed up the slope. The sixth gun was
sent to the rear for repairs – its axle was broken.[16]

Upon reaching the heights, the men spent the next two hours
inspecting the positions that they had shelled all morning – seeing

---

[13] Vaughn letters.

[14] "J.W.C." letter, *Auburn A and U.*

[15] *Ibid; O.R.*, Vol. 25, Part I, 612. The reprinted letter by "J.W.C." referred to the soldier as "Corporal Dempay," but must have meant
Dempsey.

[16] *Ibid.*

firsthand the damage they had inflicted on the enemy artillery. A member of the unit gave the following description.

> **Three brass twelve pounders, were left in these forts, with the limber chest we exploded, and three others. Several dead men and horses lay about.**
> **They left the guns without spiking them.** [17]

At 3:15 the battery was ordered to follow the Second Brigade of Brigadier General Albion Howe's division, as they headed west on the Plank Road. Sedgwick directed the Sixth Corps toward Lee's position, following Hooker's instructions. Unknown to the general, however, was the fact that Hooker had previously ordered his troops near Chancellorsville to retire; thus allowing Lee to turn the bulk of his forces on Sedgwick's command.

Brigadier General William Brooks' First Division proceeded down the Plank Road, until they made contact with Brigadier General Cadimus Wilcox's Alabama Brigade – which was deployed to protect against such an advance. The two forces soon became involved in a heated exchange. In the mean time, Major General Lafayette McLaws' division, which had previously been ordered from its place in line near Chancellorsville, was quickly moving to assist Wilcox.

Still unaware of Hooker's misfortune, General Sedgwick assumed the bulk of the Confederate army was far from his front. It was not until late in the afternoon that the general became suspicious of trouble; the opposition steadily increased on his front, and then the rebels launched an attack. Now, rather than planning an advance, the general was forced to make preparations for defense.

Part of General Sedgwick's measures included artillery support, and several batteries (including Cowan's) were ordered to the front. Cowan's guns rolled forward to a place where the road passed through a clearing. The guns were pulled off the right side

---

[17] "J.W.C." letter, *Auburn A and U; O.R.*, Vol. 25, Part I, 612. Spiking the guns was a method of temporarily rendering the piece unserviceable, which would have prevented the Federals from using them.

of the road and came into battery with a fine field of fire to their front. From here they could open on any troops that emerged from the woods 700 yards away.[18] While these five pieces were supporting the infantry, the gun which was sent to the rear embarked on a memorable adventure.

Lieutenant Theodore Atkins had previously taken the disabled piece back across the river for repairs. After working all afternoon to replace the broken axle, Lieutenant Atkins finally led the gun and the unit's supply and repair wagons across the bridge. Upon reaching the heights they noticed that Captain Cowan and the battery were nowhere to be found. Naturally assuming they followed the division, the lieutenant decided to proceed in the same direction. Unfortunately, Atkins received some misinformation as to which road to take, thus the cannon and wagons started down the wrong road. After riding about a mile the lieutenant became suspicious. He halted the wagons, and took Sergeant Sears with him to investigate. Following the road a short distance they saw some pickets.

One of the soldiers jumped to his feet and shouted, "Is the enemy coming?"

Lieutenant Atkins recognized the man as a Confederate and responded, "Yes!"

His ploy didn't work, however, and the soldier cried, "I know who you are, you're the enemy!"

The man panicked, giving Atkins and Sears an opportunity to escape. The two wheeled about and headed back to the wagons as fast as their horses would carry them.

Galloping up to the head of their small train, they shouted orders to change direction. The crews managed to turn all of the teams around, and as they started back down the road artillery shells began bursting around them. The animals galloped away from the danger until they were forced to make an abrupt halt; a tree fell in their path. Some of the men dismounted, trying to lead the animals around the obstruction. The wagon mules panicked, and quickly entangled themselves in the fallen branches. The teamsters decided they would have to cut one of the animals loose,

---

[18] *O.R.*, Vol. 25, Part I, 612.

but as they tried the entire team broke free and ran off. Atkins and his troops managed to extricate the artillery piece, but their forge and three other wagons had to be abandoned. Disappointed, the lieutenant returned to the battery and informed Captain Cowan as to their loss.[19]

The following morning, May 4, Cowan's position remained relatively quiet; the only activity occurred when some of the enemy troops attempted to build defensive works by using planks from the road.[20] Cowan's pieces fired several shells in their direction, greatly discouraging these efforts. As the morning passed to afternoon, the butternut and gray soldiers began to probe the Federal lines in preparation for a major assault. The Union troops anxiously waited for the attack, which finally began at 5:30 p.m.[21]

The Confederate effort quickly gained ground, and General Sedgwick decided to withdraw his forces toward Scott's Ford. He went forward and informed Captain Cowan that the battery needed to hold its position as long as possible, at least until General Brooks' troops passed beyond the battery. Cowan's gunners held out for forty-five minutes, firing canister at the advancing skirmishers. Finally, alone and in danger of being surrounded, Cowan gave the order to retire.[22]

The captain decided to withdraw the battery one piece at a time. By doing so the retiring cannon would have the benefit of cover fire from the other guns. He instructed the crew servicing the farthest piece on the right to retire first.

Giving the order to load, gun after gun was fired, then immediately limbered up and started down the road, and before the last

---

[19] *O.R.*, Vol. 25, Part I, 613; "J.W.C." letter, *Auburn A and U.*

[20] The Plank Road was constructed of planks that helped prevent the animals and wheels from sinking in the mud.

[21] *O.R.*, Vol. 25, Part I, 612; *West Point Atlas*, Map 90.

[22] *O.R.*, Vol. 25, Part I, 613. "General Sedgwick informed me that he was about to withdraw the infantry, and ordered me to hold my position as long as possible, holding on until General Brooks passed, if I could. Harn's battery, on my left [and a regiment]...remain[ed] at this point at 7 p.m. I continued to fire into the enemy's lines until 7:30 p.m."

> shell had exploded and the smoke cleared we
> were several rods away. [23]

The six cannon rumbled down the road toward the ford and the safety of their lines. Upon arriving at the Sixth Corps defensive perimeter near the river, the roll was taken – all were present and accounted for. The men then waited in this position until it was their turn to cross the bridge and reached the safety of the other side.

> At 9:00 o'clock we were at the Ford; here we
> stood nearly four hours, waiting orders to
> cross, while every few minutes a shell ex-
> ploded on or near the bridge, a few yards dis-
> tant. At one o'clock A.M. we were ordered
> over the river, and had just crossed when two
> shells exploded on the middle of the bridge
> where two minutes before our Battery had
> passed. [24]

During the Battle of Chancellorsville Cowan's battery per-
formed superbly. They received compliments from General Sedgwick and many of those who fought near them. The men were
proud of this fact, as the following letter excerpts reveal.

> Cowan's battery is praised by everybody
> who saw it fight, from Gen. Sedgwick down,
> and I am happy to state not a man was hurt.
> One man had a ball through his coat, how-
> ever. [25]

> One thing you need not fear. That is that
> our Battery will ever shirk its duty. It has re-
> ceived the compliments of [General Sedgwick]
> for the excellent service it rendered... [26]

---

[23] "J.W.C." letter, *Auburn A and U; O.R.,* Vol. 25, Part I, 613.
[24] "J.W.C." letter, *Auburn A and U.*
[25] *Ibid.*
[26] Vaughn letters

Chapter Six

"Our Friends Were

Waiting for Us"

After the Battle of Chancellorsville, General Lee and his Army of Northern Virginia rode high on a feeling of invincibility. Lee's confidence in his men, coupled with the rare opportunity to grasp the initiative, encouraged him to invade the North while the Army of the Potomac recovered from defeat. Thus, in early June, he set his forces in motion toward Maryland.

News of the invasion had a strange effect on the Federal troops – for many, it actually improved their morale. Rather than focusing on the recent defeat at Chancellorsville, the Union soldiers became invigorated at the prospect of fighting an enemy on familiar ground. Suddenly *they* were the inspired defenders protecting homes and families, and the Confederates had to shoulder the burden of being the invaders. Sergeant Henry Vaughn's letter home was typical of those written during this period.

[Chancellorsville] **has played out but the Union and the Love of the Union still live in the**

hearts of its brave defenders...[We are] glad that Lee has taken the offensive. We know that it will cost many of us our heart's blood – but we know that we can whip him – most everlasting whip him, now.[1]

General Joseph Hooker responded to the enemy's advance with signs of aggression. The Union commander wanted to attack Lee's rear as he moved, or strike south toward Richmond, but Lincoln and Halleck overruled him. The general's performance at Chancellorsville did little to give the president confidence in such risky actions. Lincoln's primary concern was to defend the cities in the North; this necessitated that Hooker move to confront the invaders.

By June 27, the bulk of the Army of the Potomac was near Frederick, Maryland. The Union cavalry scouted toward Emmitsburg, Maryland and Gettysburg, Pennsylvania, in an effort to locate Lee's army.[2]

President Lincoln, meanwhile, became increasingly concerned. The fear of another psychological collapse by Hooker weighed heavily on his mind, especially as Hooker showed signs of succumbing to paranoia – he began inflating the size of the enemy forces and clamoring for more troops. Lincoln preferred to remove Hooker from command, but hesitated to do so because of the potential adverse effects on the army's morale (and possible political repercussions from Hooker's friends in Congress). Fortunately for the president, the general provided him with a way out.

Joseph Hooker and General Halleck became involved in a dispute concerning the garrison at Harper's Ferry. General Hooker wanted to evacuate the position while Halleck insisted the force stay as a threat to Lee's line of communication. "Fighting Joe" hoped to pressure Halleck by offering to resign – which under the

---

[1] Vaughn letters; McPherson, *Battle Cry of Freedom,* 652. McPherson quotes a Federal officer who wrote, "The idea that Pennsylvania is invaded and that we are fighting on our own soil proper, influences them [the Federal soldiers] strongly. They are more determined than I have ever seen them before."

[2] *West Point Atlas*, 94

circumstances Hooker never dreamed would be accepted. Lincoln, however, saw this as an excellent opportunity to be rid of the general without forcing him out. The president quickly accepted Hooker's resignation and selected Major General George G. Meade as his successor.

General Meade took command on June 28, and started the Army of the Potomac moving north the following day. He sent Major General John Reynolds with three corps (the First, Third, and Eleventh) ahead toward Gettysburg. Meade then made preparations for the rest of the army to follow.

As Reynolds moved the vanguard of the army north, the Sixth Corps (to which Cowan's battery was assigned) remained behind at Manchester, Maryland, to pull in their scattered columns. Before bivouacking at Manchester the battery had experienced five days of hard marching. On the 26th they left camp near Fairfax, Virginia, and headed toward Chantilly. By the 27th they crossed the Potomac at Edward's Ferry and continued on to Frederick, Maryland. From Frederick they marched north to Manchester, where they established camp at 6 p.m. on July 1st.[3]

The Sixth was the largest of the seven infantry corps in the Army of the Potomac.[4] The corps commander, Major General John Sedgwick, assembled his troops and awaited orders. General Sedgwick was a graduate of the United States Military Academy and a veteran of the war with Mexico. An excellent commander, he was much beloved by his men.

On the same day the Sixth Corps was at Manchester, the lead elements of the Army of the Potomac first engaged the Confederates at Gettysburg. General Reynolds led the First Corps onto the fields west of the village, where they met Major General Henry Heth's troops. The fighting quickly escalated, and the Federal Eleventh Corps moved through Gettysburg to engage Lieutenant

---

[3] "J.W.C." letter, dated July 4, 1863, *Auburn A and U*; Andrew Cowan's account of the battle in, "When Cowan's Battery Withstood Pickett's Splendid Charge," in the New York *Herald*, July 2, 1911. Cited hereinafter as Cowan, *Herald* account, July 1911.

[4] John W. Busey and David Martin, *Regimental Strengths and Losses at Gettysburg* (Longstreet House, 1986), 16. Mr. Busey and Martin's excellent work lists the Sixth Corps as the largest, with over 15,000 men.

General Richard S. Ewell's Corps north of town. Late in the day the Southern forces coordinated their efforts and drove the Federals back through the village – but the precious time the two Union corps bought allowed the Federals to hold the strategic Cemetery Hill until the remainder of the Army of the Potomac arrived.

News of these events traveled slowly (by our twentieth century standards). On the evening of July 1, Captain Cowan and the other officers in the Sixth Corps had no idea of what had happened at Gettysburg. In fact, Cowan and First Lieutenant William H. Johnson accepted an invitation for dinner in Manchester. The ladies of the city provided a buffet supper of chicken and other home cooked dishes in honor of the Federal troops camped nearby. Before the officers left, however, they gave instructions to notify them immediately if there were any developments.[5]

When Cowan and Johnson entered the banquet hall a young lady met them at the door. Their hostess escorted the officers toward the long tables of food while engaging them in friendly conversation. As the three stood in line chatting, a messenger from the battery galloped into town. Dismounting from his winded horse, he rushed to find the two officers. Upon entering the hall, he soon caught sight of Cowan and informed the captain that the battery had received marching orders. Cowan thanked his hostess for her hospitality, but said they would have to leave. The young lady grabbed a bottle of wine from the table and gave it to him as he rushed out. Cowan stuffed the bottle into his saddlebag and rode off with all haste to catch the battery.[6]

The two artillery officers were not the only soldiers hurrying back to their units. When the Sixth Corps received word of the engagement at Gettysburg (along with the heartbreaking news of General Reynolds' death), the whole command quickly prepared to march.

Cowan described their initial movements.

---

[5] Andrew Cowan's address for the "Opening of the Military day meeting". The exact location of this meeting is unclear, but part of the speech was reprinted in the *Louisville Courier Journal*, July 10, 1913. Cited hereinafter as Cowan's "Military day address."

[6] *Ibid.*

> **At nine o'clock P.M., we were again on the march, headed for Gettysburg. Our movement was slow and tedious throughout the night, on account of the movements of the other troops or trains ahead of us.**[7]

Sedgwick's soldiers soon encountered a problem. General Meade had ordered the army supply trains to backtrack in an effort to ensure their safety. These wagons cluttered the road, creating a serious delay. The general sent officers ahead to clear the path, and the wagons were ushered off the road so the Sixth Corps could pass.[8]

The march during the night was very intense. Rumors of the day's fighting at Gettysburg circulated up and down the lines. The information was inconclusive about the outcome of the engagement, but the necessity of the Sixth Corps' presence was clear.

In many ways the darkness made the march more difficult (mainly finding the right roads in the dark), but the soldiers welcomed the relief from the heat. They continued on through the night, resting but a few minutes each hour. Finally, near daybreak, the men fell out for half an hour to eat some breakfast.[9]

Cowan later recalled the events after they resumed their march.

> **...soon after sunrise our march up the Baltimore turnpike in the direction of the battlefield became a race, urged forward by the officers and inspired later by the sound of cannon far ahead. The heat was fierce and the road very dusty...**[10]

---

[7] Cowan, *Herald* account, July, 1911; *O.R.*, Vol. 27, Part One, 665. The original destination apparently was Taneytown, Maryland, but then the corps received orders "directing it to proceed by rapid marches to Gettysburg."

[8] Glenn Tucker, *High Tide at Gettysburg* (Bobbs- Merrill, 1958), 206.

[9] Edwin B. Coddington, *The Gettysburg Campaign* (New York, 1968), 357; *O.R.,* Vol. 27, Part One, 665.

[10] Cowan, *Herald* account, July 1911.

Another member of the Sixth Corps remembers the events as follows:

> **At the houses on the roadsides, the citizens, their wives and daughters, were bringing water, from which the soldiers filled their canteens as they passed. At Littletown we saw citizens bringing the wounded from the field in carriages...The marching was more rapid. Our friends were waiting for us.**[11]

Stirred on by the proximity of battle, the men of the Sixth Corps quickened their steps and pressed on toward Gettysburg. They endured a grueling march of approximately thirty-four miles, finally arriving on the field late on July 2.[12] Cowan's battery was near the front of the advancing Sixth Corps column, just behind the lead brigade. When they crossed the bridge over Rock Creek, Cowan's guns were ordered into a field on the left of the road to allow the infantry to advance.[13] Several of the Sixth Corps units pressed on toward Little Round Top, shoring up the lines in this key position.[14]

As the other artillery units arrived, they joined Cowan's guns to the left of the road. The batteries were placed in line to form a defensive barrier against an assault from the army's left.[15]

Andrew Cowan later remembered the scene.

> [While we remained in this position,] **the road became crowded with ambulances, passing**

---

[11] George T. Stevens, *Three Years in the Sixth Corps* (Albany, 1866), 240.

[12] Stevens, *Three Years in the Sixth Corps,* 241. Mr. Stevens, who was a surgeon in the 77th New York Infantry, stated, "It was five o'clock when the Sixth Corps arrived on the battlefield, having made an unprecedented march of thirty-four miles."

[13] Cowan, *Herald* account, July, 1911.

[14] O.R., Vol. 27, Part One, 663.

[15] Cowan, *Herald* account, July, 1911; William F. Fox, ed. *New York at Gettysburg*, 3 Vols. (Albany, 1900), 1276. Cited hereinafter as *New York at Gettysburg*.

from the fighting ground to the rear, loaded with the wounded and followed by hundreds of others who were able to walk and by many stragglers, the riff raff in the rear of a battle. It was not an inspiring spectacle; besides, a rumor that the army would retreat that night and that the Sixth Corps would be the rear guard was whispered about.[16]

Colonel Charles Tompkins, the commander of the Sixth Corps artillery, rode from battery to battery making sure all the guns were in position and ready for action if necessary. The men of the 1st Independent Battery remained at their posts and listened to the sounds of battle. As the sun began to set, and the fighting subsided, the weary cannoneers became more at ease. Colonel Tompkins ordered Cowan to have his men stay alert and in position during the night.[17]

The preceding thirty-six hours had been exhausting for the men of the 1st New York Independent Battery. They had experienced an incredible march, much of it in the dark and at a rapid pace. And now they would spend another evening without sleep. Unfortunately this night with little rest came before one of their toughest days of fighting of the entire war.

[16] Cowan, *Herald* account, July, 1911.
[17] *Ibid.*

Chapter Seven

"I will show you

the situation"

The results of the first two days of battle at Gettysburg were indecisive. On the first day, July 1, the Confederates won the field, but the Federals achieved their goal of holding Cemetery Hill. On the second day the Southern offensive nearly overran the Federal left, but the determined Union troops managed to hold on. By the end of July 2, both armies were bloodied, but poised and ready to decide the fate of the battle, and possibly the war.

The roles for the two opposing armies on the third day of battle were firmly established; the Federals would remain the defenders, while the Confederates continued on the offensive. During the evening and early morning hours Lee made plans to strike the Union position. At the same time, General Meade and his corps commanders made arrangements to adjust their defenses for Lee's expected attack.

In order to bolster the Federal defenses, some of the Sixth Corps artillery and infantry units were temporarily distributed to other commands. Meade's position was roughly the shape of a fishhook; The Eleventh, Twelfth and part of the First Corps formed the hook at Cemetery and Culp's Hills, the Second and remnants of the First Corps held the center, while the Third and Fifth Corps anchored the southern end of the line at the Round Tops. The remainder of the Sixth Corps guarded the rear of the Round Tops, to protect the army's left flank from attack.

The sunrise on July 3, illuminated the movements of couriers who carried orders and instructions to different commands. One of these riders, an aid from the First Corps headquarters, approached the row of Sixth Corps artillery and spoke with Colonel Tompkins. Soon after their conversation Captain Cowan was instructed to prepare his battery to report to the First Corps.

Orders were shouted and the cannoneers scrambled to ready their guns for movement. With the cannon limbered, the unit followed the officer. Captain Cowan later described the movement.

> **We marched across the bridge and up the Baltimore road to the first road turning to our left, which the staff officer guiding us told me led to the Taneytown road in the rear of the northern edge of the Little Round Top.[1]**

The battery approached the Taneytown road and halted. Captain Cowan instructed the men to remain there while he rode forward to get their orders. Spurring his mount toward a grove of trees where a "First Corps" flag was gently flying, he hoped to find Major General John Newton. Cowan rode up to the officer's tent, and inquired as to where he might find General Newton (who had just taken command of the First Corps).[2]

---

[1] Cowan, *Herald* account, July, 1911.

[2] Cowan to Nicholson letters. Collection of letters written by Andrew Cowan to Colonel John P. Nicholson, Chairman of the Gettysburg National Park Commission. Four letters: copies of three are in the Gettysburg National Military Park Library, the fourth in the Special Collections of the Colgate University Library. Cited hereinafter as Cowan to Nicholson; Cowan, *Herald* account, July, 1911; *O.R.*, Vol. 27, Part One, 690; *New York at Gettysburg*, 1276.

Major General Abner Doubleday was the officer who greeted the captain. Cowan informed General Doubleday that his battery was temporarily assigned to the First Corps, and inquired as to General Newton's orders. Doubleday told Cowan that General Newton was inspecting the lines, and doubted if an additional battery was needed.

"Come with me, Captain," Doubleday said after noting the disappointment on Cowan's face, "and I will show you the situation."[3]

Cowan remained on his horse and followed as the general walked through the grove to the First Corps lines. The young artilleryman noticed the Federal defensive dispositions, and then looked across the fields where he saw the Confederates on Seminary Ridge.

"You see if I send your battery in now," said Doubleday, "it would draw the fire of all the guns along yonder ridge."

Doubleday briefly explained the problems this fire would cause for the infantry, and then said, "Park your battery at some convenient place. Let your men get their breakfasts, send me word where you are, and when I can use you, I will send for you."[4]

Cowan rode back to the battery and ordered the unit out into the field beside the intersection. After the limbers, guns, and caissons made their way into the narrow clearing, the men began caring for the animals. Soon fires were started and the smell of coffee filled the air. The men noticed the trees at the end of the field, which would provide excellent shade for a nap.

Once the battery was situated, Captain Cowan called for his bugler, Sergeant Lewis Tallman, and together they rode toward the front. Cowan led them to the First Corps line, and then north along Cemetery Ridge. There was a definite possibility his battery might see action somewhere on this ground, so the captain wanted to have a better look at it.

Cowan turned his keen eyes toward the Confederate guns across the field, and made a mental note of the distances. The two continued scouting the Union lines all the way to a small clump of

---

[3] Cowan, *Herald* account, July, 1911.
[4] *Ibid.*

trees in the center of the Second Corps line. After this inspection, Cowan and Tallman headed back to the battery.

Upon returning to camp they found the men settling in for a much-deserved rest. The captain also welcomed the opportunity for sleep and, after making arrangements for his horse, spread his coat on the ground and lay down to take a nap. Unfortunately, this rest would be very short.[5]

Across the fields on Seminary Ridge, a row of Confederate artillery pieces prepared to open fire on the center of the Federal line. Earlier in the day General Lee had hoped to attack the flanks of Meade's position, but with the dispositions for this action not being met, he was forced to change his plans.[6]   His new plan called for a major assault against the Federal center, with the focal point being the same small clump of trees which Cowan and Tallman noticed on their inspection ride.

In preparation for the attack, General Lee called for nearly one hundred and sixty artillery pieces to focus a barrage on the center of the Federal line. Their mission was to damage the batteries and weaken the infantry positions – both materially and psychologically. The plan also called for a number of Confederate guns to advance just behind the infantry, so as to protect the advancing infantry's exposed flanks.[7]

At approximately 1:00 in the afternoon, the signal was given and the Confederate guns erupted.[8] The shells quickly crashed into

---

[5] Cowan, *Herald* account, July, 1911. It is important to note that Captain Cowan rode forward and informed General Newton of his position sometime before his "rest" (*O.R.*, Vol. 27, Part 1, 690), but there is *no evidence* in Cowan's writings that the battery moved from this field until the cannonade started.

[6] Coddington, *The Gettysburg Campaign*, 458. "Now that a well-coordinated attack at an early hour was no longer possible...because Longstreet failed to bring Pickett's division up early enough...Lee had to scrap his plans for the day and start all over again." Thus his next choice was the frontal assault, Pickett's charge.

[7] *West Point Atlas*, 98; Coddington, *The Gettysburg Campaign*, 462.

[8] Coddington, *The Gettysburg Campaign*, 493; *West Point Atlas*, 98; *O.R.*, Vol. 27, Part 2, 320.

the First and Second Corps positions. Many of the fieldpieces were aimed too high, however, and their projectiles sailed over the lines and fell in the rear areas – such as the field where Cowan's men and horses were resting.[9]

As Cowan lay napping in the shade, a Confederate shell screamed over head and crashed into the trees. The captain sprang to his feet, looked around, and then shouted for the bugler to bring his horse. The mounted Tallman raced toward Cowan with the captain's horse in tow. Just as he stopped and handed Cowan the reins, Tallman's horse was struck by a projectile and fell dead under him.[10] Fortunately Tallman was not hurt.

"Stand to horse!" shouted Cowan, "Cannoneers to your posts!" With this the men rushed to their positions and prepared to move.[11] Moments later, additional commands sent the limbers toward the road. Upon reaching the intersection the men halted, and anxiously waited for further orders. While standing in the road, the horses began suffering from the fire.[12] Not only did the projectiles themselves inflict losses, but the nervous animals had to be calmed in an effort to prevent them from injuring each other.

For the men of the 1st New York Independent Battery, their involvement in the battle of Gettysburg had just begun.

---

[9] George R. Stewart, *Pickett's Charge: A Microhistory of the Final Attack at Gettysburg, July 3, 1863* (Boston, 1959), 132.

[10] Cowan, *Herald* account, July, 1911.

[11] *Ibid.*

[12] *O.R.*, Vol. 27, Part 1, 690.

Chapter Eight

"Move Up at a Gallop!"

While Captain Cowan and his men waited in the intersection for orders from the First Corps, an aide from Brigadier General Henry Hunt's staff approached the battery. This officer, Lieutenant Colonel E. R. Warner, instructed Cowan to bring the battery forward. The captain shouted commands to the drivers who turned the teams to follow the colonel.[1]

The officer led the battery toward the First Corps lines, passing through the grove near General Newton's headquarters. As they did, Cowan directed the caissons to pull off into the field.[2] The explosive cargo would be safer here, under cover, and the limbers could be brought up later to replenish the depleted ammunition chests at the front.

Once the six guns cleared the grove, they turned right and broke into a brisk trot, the horses pounding the sod as they raced behind the line of infantry. "That ride," remembered Cowan, "under such a storm of missiles, was thrilling."[3]

The shells flying over head and exploding made the ride more than "thrilling," it was extremely dangerous. As the battery was coming into position a shell burst, sending a fragment deep into

---

[1] Cowan to Nicholson; Cowan, *Herald* account, July,1911.
[2] Cowan to Nicholson.
[3] Cowan, *Herald* account, July, 1911.

Private Henry Hitchcock's thigh. The wound proved to be mortal – he died in an army hospital that evening.[4]

Colonel Warner rode to the end of the First Corps line and directed Cowan to place his pieces beside the other batteries.[5] Scrambling to their assignments, the men unhitched the guns from the limbers and grabbed the implements for loading the cannon.

Private George Brockway described this action.

> [We] **found the fire uncommonly hot but spouted away. It was but a short time before it became hot hotter hottest...the fragments came in all directions, several which called for me and one of which struck a bag of oats that was lashed to the limber (to feed at night) near where I was busy within a foot (of my head).**[6]

During the firing Private Otis C. Billings approached Cowan. "Captain," he said, "I am very sick today, please let me go back to the caissons."

The captain knew Billings was no shirker, and since he looked "pale as a ghost," it was obvious that he indeed was ill.

"No, Billings," replied Cowan sharply, "this is no time to be sick." Unfortunately the circumstances called for every man who could stand to stay at his post. Billings returned to his crew and faithfully manned his gun.[7]

Cowan's previous scouting of this line now paid off. He shouted orders and the gun crews adjusted the elevation on their pieces accordingly.

---

[4] George Brockway letter, part of the House family collection; John W. Busey, *These Honored Dead*: The Union Casualties at Gettysburg (New Jersey, 1988), 173.

[5] Cowan, *Herald* account July, 1911; Cowan to Nicholson; *New York at Gettysburg*, 1276.

[6] Brockway letter.

[7] Cowan, *Herald* account July, 1911.

We opened fire at once, [remembered Cowan] directing our aim to the left oblique, where I had previously thought we might get the best work. We fired very slowly, but there was a tremendous waste of ammunition going on. We had been trained under Captain...Romeyn B. Ayres, chief of artillery of Smith's division...to make every shot tell if possible and to never get excited.[8]

Under the tutelage of the West Point schooled Ayres, Cowan learned the importance of firing his pieces slowly and deliberately. This not only conserved ammunition, but more important it increased the accuracy of their firing. After each discharge the piece recoiled and had to be re-aimed. Rushing this process led to inaccuracy; additionally, the gunner who aimed the piece would have his vision obscured by the smoke from the previous discharge. The faster the pieces fired, the more smoke remained to obscure his vision. [9]

Cowan's deliberate discharges must have pleased the army's chief of artillery, General Henry Hunt, who rode along the line directing the fire of the batteries. Hunt realized that the Confederate cannonade was in preparation for a major assault, thus, it was imperative that his guns conserve their ammunition for the approaching infantry.

For a little more than an hour Cowan's men fired over the Emmitsburg road toward the line of Confederate artillery. Unknown to the captain or his cannoneers was the fact that a regiment heavily numbered with recruits from Auburn and Cayuga County, had fought over this same ground the previous evening. As the sun was setting on July 2nd, the 111th New York Volunteers were sent into a gap in the Union lines. They charged out to

---

[8] Cowan, *Herald* account, July, 1911.
[9] Coddington, *The Gettysburg Campaign*, 479; Cowan, *Herald* account, July, 1911. "We had been trained under Captain...Ayres...on the Peninsula and the Antietam Campaign to make every shot tell if possible and never get too excited."

meet the attacking Confederates, and helped drive them back to the Emmitsburg Road.[10]

During the cannonade the artillerymen occupied themselves with their duties, focusing on their assignments rather than the danger. The drivers, however, were not as fortunate. They had "nothing to do but stand and hold their horses," noted Cowan. And to them, the time "must have seemed an eternity."[11]

Private George Brockway, who was the number six man of his crew, stood at his limber cutting fuses as per the directives of the gunner. While performing his duty, a wounded man approached and asked for help. Brockway remembered…

> [A wounded sergeant] **came to me** [as] **I was preparing shells and wanted me to carry him off the field when the hospital was in sight and he was just as able to run as I was to carry him and more to. When** [I refused to leave my post, he reluctantly headed toward the rear]**….I looked in the direction of the hospital and I saw him a going as fast as his old legs would carry him and that was no foolish gait either. Ever and anow he would fall and then raise and go like the Devil again.**[12]

Before long, Cowan noticed his ammunition chests were being depleted (each gun having fired 45 rounds). A rider sped back to the caissons with orders to bring some of the limbers forward. While the limbers were on their way, the captain noticed an officer approaching his battery.[13]

---

[10] R.L. Murray, *The Redemption of the "Harper's Ferry Cowards": The Story of the 111th and the 126th New York State Volunteer Regiments at Gettysburg* (Wolcott, New York, 1994), 91 – 114. (They were part of Willard's Brigade).

[11] Cowan, *Herald* account, July, 1911.

[12] Brockway letter.

[13] Cowan to Nicholson 12/19/1919; Cowan, *Herald* account, July, 1911.

"Cease firing," the officer yelled. "Hold your fire for the infantry."[14]

Confused by the statement, Cowan reluctantly gave the order to cease-fire. The captain had no idea what the officer was talking about – the smoke in front of his position was so thick he could no longer see the Confederate lines.[15] For a time Cowan and his crews remained idle. Passively standing by in the midst of a cannonade, however, did not set well with Cowan or his men. Finally, with no apparent reason for the cease-fire, and with the frustration of doing nothing increasing, Cowan prepared to resume firing. Suddenly another mounted officer appeared.

"Report to General Webb at the right with your battery," the man called.[16]

The officer pointed toward the position occupied by the Second Corps. Cowan momentarily paused to assess the situation. His battery was assigned to the First Corps, thus, he did not know about leaving his place in line without permission. Glancing toward the small clump of trees on the ridge, the young artilleryman saw Brigadier General Alexander Webb waving his hat.[17] Behind the general some field pieces were limping off to the rear. Instantly Cowan understood the situation; his guns were needed to fill the gap created by a retiring battery.

---

[14]Cowan to Nicholson 12/19/1919.

[15]*Ibid*. Cowan explained, "I did not know what was meant by 'the infantry,' but ceased firing immediately." It was only after Cowan moved to the right that he saw the Confederate infantry. "The smoke cleared away as I rode up [to Webb's position], & I caught sight of the rebel flags far beyond the Emmitsburg road, & knew what was meant by holding my fire for the infantry."

[16]Cowan to Nicholson; Andrew Cowan to Colonel John B. Bachelder. Originals letters contained in the New Hampshire Historical Society. Reprinted in, *The Bachelder Papers: Gettysburg in Their Own Words*, Three Volumes. David L. and Audrey J. Ladd, eds. (Dayton, Ohio, 1994), 281. Cited hereinafter as *Bachelder Papers*; *New York at Gettysburg*, 1276. The officer was probably Captain Charles H. Banes, *Bachelder Papers*, 1702.

[17]Cowan to Nicholson; Cowan, *Herald* account, July, 1911; *New York at Gettysburg*, 1276.

"Limber to the right," bellowed Cowan. "Move up at a gallop!"[18]

With this order Captain Cowan assured himself and his battery a place in Gettysburg's history.

---

[18]Cowan to Nicholson.

Chapter Nine

"Fire from all other parts

of the

Federal line slackened"

[Note: This chapter is an overview of the action during the cannonade, thus it backtracks in time slightly. This is necessary to get a better understanding of the events pertaining to Cowan's battery.]

At the beginning of the cannonade on July 3, the Second Corps had five artillery batteries in position at the center of the Federal line. At the northernmost part of the line was the 1st United States, Battery I, under the command of Lieutenant George Woodruff. Next was Captain William Arnold's 1st Rhode Island Light, Battery A. Just north of the small clump of trees, at the point where the stone wall formed a right angle, was the 4th United States, Battery A, under the command of a twenty-two year old New Yorker named Alonzo Cushing. On the south side of the trees was another Rhode Island unit, 1st Rhode Island Light, Battery B. And finally, just south of the Rhode Islanders was the 1st New York Light, Battery B, under the command of Captain James McKay Rorty.

Captain Rorty had only joined Battery B, the previous day (July 2). Rorty was assigned to command the battery because Captain Rufus D. Pettit, who led the unit during the first two years of service, had recently resigned his commission. Battery B was a veteran group, having fought through the early campaigns on the Peninsula, Antietam, Fredericksburg, and Chancellorsville. Forming their ranks were men from Onondaga County, in central New York.[1]

Early on the morning of July 3, the Second Corps position near the clump of trees remained relatively quiet. As the early morning passed, however, the Federals began noticing some increasing activity among the gun crews in the rebel lines. Suddenly, around 8:00 o'clock some of the Confederate pieces opened a short concentrated fire on the Second Corps position.[2] At least one of the shells found its mark, causing an explosion among Cushing's artillery limbers.[3] The Federal guns quickly replied, which quieted the Southern batteries.

The late morning hours of July 3, were ones of relative inactivity and silence. One officer in the Second Corps commented that this period seemed "as quiet as the Sabbath day."[4] Many of

---

[1] *New York at Gettysburg*, 1182; Brian C. Pohanka, "James McKay Rorty: A Worthy Officer, A Gallant Soldier, An Estimable Man." Manuscript in the Gettysburg National Military Park Library. The Onondaga battery was one of several Second Corps units that were involved in the repulse of the Confederate charge on the evening of July 2nd. Battery B was heavily engaged and lost one man killed, eight wounded, and had thirteen horses disabled. The 1st Rhode Island, Battery B, also suffered greatly – the casualties included one man killed, nine missing or wounded, with their commander, Lieutenant T. Fred Brown, being severely wounded in the neck. *O.R.*, Vol. 27, Part I, 478.

[2] *Ibid*; Naiawald, *Grape and Canister*, 418.

[3] Kent Masterson Brown, *Cushing of Gettysburg: The Story of a Union Artillery Commander* (University of Kentucky, 1993), 224.

[4] Murray, *Redemption of the "Harper's Ferry Cowards,"*124.

the men took advantage of the lull by trying to find some food and water. The quiet proved merely to be the calm before the storm.

At approximately 1:00 p.m., some of the Union soldiers noticed a puff of smoke emerge from one of the guns on Seminary Ridge. Soon another was spotted, which was quickly followed by an eruption from the entire line. The focal point of the bombardment turned out to be the artillery and infantry of the Second Corps. Shells from over one hundred and fifty Confederate pieces soon began bursting among the Union troops on the ridge, sending soldiers scurrying for cover. Unfortunately, the Union artillerymen were not afforded the same opportunity for protection as the infantry – they manned their guns out in the open.

For the first fifteen minutes of the cannonade the batteries of the Second Corps remained silent. Anxious cannoneers wanted to return fire, but they were under orders from the chief of artillery not to do so. General Hunt believed it was more important for the Union batteries to save their ammunition for the infantry assault.[5]

Major General Winfield Scott Hancock was of a decidedly different opinion than Hunt. As the commander of the Second Corps, Hancock believed the guns should have immediately replied to the Confederate fire, so as to reassure his troops. He was concerned about the men's frame of mind; the soldiers might become demoralized unless they could see the Federal artillery replying to the cannonade. Consequently, Hancock countermanded Hunt's orders and told the artillery officers in several batteries to begin firing at the Confederates.[6]

---

[5] Robert U. Johnson and Clarence C. Buel, eds. *Battles and Leaders of the Civil War*, 4 vols. (New York, 1884 - 1888), vol. III, 372. Cited hereinafter as *Battles and Leaders*. Hunt had previously interpreted the massing of Confederate artillery as an indication of a pre-assault cannonade to "crush our batteries and shake our infantry; at least to cause us to exhaust our ammunition in reply..." He wanted the artillery to maximize their fire against the approaching Confederate infantry, thus he "instructed the chiefs of artillery and battery commanders to withhold their fire for fifteen or twenty minutes after the cannonade commenced, so that...we should have sufficient [ammunition] left to meet the assault."

[6] Naiawald, *Grape and Canister*, 420; Stewart, *Pickett's Charge*, 136; *Battles and Leaders,* Vol. III, 372.

During this gale of fire Hancock's batteries suffered terribly – especially Brown's 1st Rhode Island, Battery B. They were already shorthanded from the heavy casualties suffered the previous evening. Thus, during the cannonade they could only man four of their six 3-inch rifles.[7]

General Hunt rode along the length of the Union lines during the cannonade, inspecting his artillery. Near the later stages of the bombardment he made his way to Cemetery Hill, which was north of the Second Corps position, hoping to find General Meade. Hunt wanted to order his artillery to cease firing, believing the tactic might draw out the Confederate infantry while the Federal guns still had ammunition.[8] Before giving such an order, however, he wanted to check with his commander.

Upon arriving at Cemetery Hill he met with Major General Oliver O. Howard, the commander of the Eleventh Corps, and his chief of artillery, Major Thomas Osborn. After General Howard informed him that Meade had just left, Hunt explained his cease-fire theory to the two officers. Howard and Osborn concurred with Hunt's theory, thus encouraging the general to send word down the line instructing the batteries to hold their fire.[9]

---

[7] Naiawald, *Grape and Canister*, 421; Stewart, *Pickett's Charge*, 147. Serving the guns amidst the hail of solid shot and shells took its toll on the crews. In Cushing's battery, for example, one of the cannoneers had his leg nearly taken off by a shell as it passed under the limber. When one of the crews in Brown's Rhode Island battery was about to load a solid shot into their 12 pound Napoleon , an enemy shell struck the muzzle of the brass tube. The explosion killed the number one man and mortally wounded the number two man. Replacements stepped forward, attempting to place the solid shot in the piece. The impact from the Confederate shell knocked the muzzle out of round, however, causing the shot to become wedged in the end. Brown's battery was now down to three serviceable pieces, as well as nearly being out of ammunition. Stewart, *Pickett's Charge*, 147.

[8] *Battles and Leaders,* Vol. III, 374.

[9] *Ibid;* Naisawald, *Grape and Canister,* 422; Edward G. Longacre, *The Man Behind the Guns: A Biography of Henry Jackson Hunt, Chief of Artillery, Army of the Potomac (New York, 1991)*, 174. In his writings, Major Osborn states that he suggested the cessation of fire. See, *The Eleventh Corps Artillery at Gettysburg: The papers of Major Thomas Ward Osborn.* Edited by Herb S. Crumb. (Hamilton, NY: 1991), 39.

When the order to cease-fire reached the batteries of the Second Corps, their effectiveness had already been greatly reduced – their long range ammunition was expended and numerous casualties had greatly reduced the crews. General Hunt later inspected this part of the line and found that the batteries were decimated. Brown's Rhode Island battery was especially hard hit. Compounding the problem was the fact that the battery had used its entire canister supply the night before, so it would be of limited effectiveness during the charge. What was left of the guns were ordered off the field.[10]

On Seminary Ridge, Colonel E. P. Alexander, the artillery officer in charge of the Confederate cannonade, carefully watched the Federal center for signs of it weakening. He was becoming increasingly anxious because his own batteries were running low on ammunition. If the Federals did not show some effects of the cannonade soon, he thought, the success of the attack would be doubtful. Thus when he noticed the Federal fire beginning to subside (as Hunt's cease-fire order spread down the line), he hoped it meant his efforts were successful. Carefully scanning the Federal lines through his field glasses he noticed that several batteries "limbered up & left and the fire from all other parts of the federal line slackened up materially."[11]

It was at this point – when the Second Corps artillery had basically fallen silent, and with the Confederate infantry beginning to emerge from the woods on Seminary Ridge – that Brown's Rhode Island battery withdrew. Seeing the emerging gray lines, General Webb felt a sense of urgency in replacing Brown's guns. He sent a staff officer to find some batteries to bolster his line.[12] Thus it was to this request that Cowan responded.

---

[10] Stewart, *Pickett's Charge*, 156 - 157; *Bachelder Papers*, 822.

[11] *Bachelder Papers*, 489.

[12] *O.R.*, Vol. 27, Part I, 428; Brown, *Cushing of Gettysburg*, 240.

Chapter Ten

"Hurrah for the Ould Flag"

"Limber to the right," bellowed Cowan. "Move up at a gallop!"[1]

Cowan's crews responded with enthusiasm. The men, many of them stripped to their shirts, dashed to hitch the guns to the limbers. Pieces in place, the men "sprang with wild cheers upon the limber chests and up on the guns, their implements which they had not time to replace, still in their hands."[2]

Turning the teams to the north, toward the small clump of trees, the drivers shouted and the animals raced forward. They "dashed at a gallop," thundering off in the direction of the motioning General Webb.[3] The excited horses quickly covered the short distance and the drivers began to slow the teams as they approached Webb's troops. The horses pulling lead gun, "Gun Number One" under the command of Sergeant Peter Mullaly, could not be slowed in time and they overshot Webb's position. Unfortunately this meant that Mullaly was forced to place his lone gun on

---

[1] Cowan to Nicholson.

[2] *Bachelder Papers*, 281; Cowan, *Herald* account, July, 1911. Cowan stated that several of the men were stripped to their skin.

[3] *Bachelder Papers*, 1146.

the other side of the copse of trees from where the other five pieces would go into action.[4]

While the 1st New York's guns were on the move, the smoky haze in front of the Second Corps lines began to clear. General Webb caught Cowan's attention as the captain shouted orders to his crew. The general pointed toward Seminary Ridge, and as Cowan peered through the clearing smoke he then understood "what was meant by holding my fire for the infantry...[He] caught sight of the rebel battle flags far beyond the Emmitsburg road."[5]

Cowan shouted additional commands to his crews, who quickly began loading the guns and adjusting elevations. With all the confusion the captain had not noticed the absence of Mullaly's gun. Now looking around he counted only five pieces. Learning his first gun was on the other side of the trees, he rode over to investigate.[6]

As Cowan approached, General Webb and Lieutenant Cushing were conferring as to the placement of Cushing's guns. Cushing saw Cowan approach, and the two briefly exchanged pleasantries. Cowan apologized for his piece crowding the lieutenant's battery. Cushing assured him that there was no problem and then turned to order his remaining pieces, "By hand to the front." The serviceable cannon of his battery moved forward to the low stone wall, where their last charges of canister were placed beside them.[7]

Cowan then gave Mullaly some instructions and returned to his other guns. As he did, the captain noticed that there were men in front of his battery, members of the 69th Pennsylvania.[8] The 69th was one of Webb's four regiments near the copse of trees.[9]

---

[4] *Bachelder Papers*, 1146.; Cowan, *Herald* account, July, 1911; Cowan to Nicholson.

[5] Cowan to Nicholson.

[6] *Ibid.*

[7] *Ibid*; *New York at Gettysburg*, 1277; Bachelder Papers, 1157; Cowan, *Herald* account, July, 1911.

[8] Companies B and K of the 69th were directly in front of Cowan's battery. The other companies were along the wall to the right. See, D. Scott Hartwig, "It Struck Horror to Us All" *The Gettysburg Magazine*, January 1, 1991, Issue Number Four, 97.

[9] *O.R.*, Vol. 27, Part I, 428, 431, 432, 433 - 435. All but two of the companies of the 106th Pennsylvania were sent to assist the Eleventh Corps

The Pennsylvanians were lying prone near the stone wall, "about thirty yards" ahead of Cowan's position.[10]

> **We opened at once and continued pouring shell upon them** [remembered Cowan]...**"**[11]
> **They came on in splendid order, closing on their left as the shot and shell ploughed gaps through their ranks, and keeping their regular formation until they had to cross fences at the Emmitsburg road. It was a wonderful sight!**[12]

The cannoneers steadily served their guns as General George Pickett's troops approached. With his pieces thundering away at the gray lines, Captain Cowan dismounted to get a better view (the best visibility was near the ground because of the smoke created by the guns).[13] Through the smoke the captain watched the Southern troops, "as they advanced in masses..."[14]

"Before crossing the road," Cowan recalled, "their lines moved as if on parade, closing to their left, evidently directed at the clump of trees in the angle."[15]

The Union infantry opened fire on the gray-clad troops as they reached the Emmitsburg road.[16] The volleys temporarily slowed the advance, but their lines reformed and pressed on. They climbed the fences on the road, and began to advance up the grad-

---

on the evening of July 2, thus they were not with the brigade during the attack on July 3.

[10] Cowan to Nicholson. The actual distance was probably greater than Cowan's estimate, more like forty yards. (See Brown, *Cushing of Gettysburg*, 240.)

[11] *Bachelder Papers*, 282.

[12] Cowan, *Herald* account, July, 1911.

[13] Cowan to Nicholson. Cowan, "I was on foot...I could see under the smoke better than above it."

[14] Cowan, *Herald* account, July, 1911.

[15] Cowan to Nicholson.

[16] Brown, *Cushing of Gettysburg*, 244.

ual slope to the low stone wall. Noting the proximity of the Confederates, Cowan shouted orders to his gunners directing them to switch to canister.[17] The loads were quickly carried from the limbers, rammed down the tubes, and fired into the oncoming troops.

About this time General Hunt rode into the battery. He stopped near Cowan and observed his guns at work. Then, as the crews were loading their third round of canister, the general yelled, "See'em! See'em! See'em!" and proceeded to empty his revolver into the mass of enemy troops.[18] Suddenly a rebel ball

---

[17] *O.R.,* Vol. 27, Part I, 690.

[18] *Bachelder Papers,* 283, 1156; Cowan to Nicholson, 12/19/1910 and 12/5/1913; Cowan, *Herald* account, July, 1911; Letter from Andrew Cowan to Alexander Webb. The letter is now part of the Alexander Stewart Webb Collection, at the Yale University Library. Copy at the Gettysburg National Military Park Library. Cited hereinafter as Cowan to Webb. Some authors have stated that this incident took place much later, when the Confederates were coming over the wall in Cowan's front. I believe that Hunt was in the battery as the Confederates crossed the Emmitsburg Road, but left well **before** the Southern troops came over the wall for the following reasons: 1) Cowan wrote, "General Hunt, who was with my battery when I opened with canister..." In his official report Cowan stated, "I commenced firing canister at 200 yards..." (*O.R.*, Vol. 27, Part I, 690.). 2) Cowan stated, "He [Hunt] emptied his pistol at the enemy as I was loading for the third round [of canister]." (Cowan to Webb) Cowan fired three rounds of canister *and then* loaded for the last double canister round. (Cowan's address at Gettysburg, July 3, 1886). "Three times you have swept the front beyond the low stone wall or fence, with canister at point blank range, and now in this supreme instant of the contest...you load every piece with *double canister* and sweep the enemy from before them at ten yards." 3) Cowan also wrote, "He [Hunt] rode up to me when Pickett's line had advanced as far as the Emmitsburg road..." (Cowan to Nicholson, 12/19/1910). 4) And finally, a careful examination of what Hunt said before leaving Cowan's position shows that he left before the Confederates came over the wall. As Hunt was riding off he warned Cowan, "Look out or you will kill our men." He was obviously referring to the Federal soldiers in front of the battery. This is the key – there were no Federal troops in Cowan's front when the Confederates came over the wall (only wounded – see later description). Since the Union troops in front of the battery were gone when the Confederates came over the wall, there would have been no reason for Hunt to say this. Even if one believes there were Federal troops still at the wall when the Confederates overran it, Hunt would not have said, "Look out or you will kill our men," because there would have been no way to discharge the canister into the group without killing their own men. If this

struck the general's horse in the head. The mount tumbled to the ground, pinning Hunt's leg under him. Cowan and some other members of the battery helped the general extricate himself. Hunt scrambled to his feet, assuring everyone he was unhurt. Captain Cowan then called for Sergeant Orasmas Van Ettan to bring his horse to the general. Hunt remounted, and as he turned to ride off yelled, "Look out or you will kill our men," (referring to the Union troops along the wall).[19]

The blasts of canister discouraged a rebel advance in front of Cowan's position. After closing to within one hundred yards of the stone wall, most of them either shifted toward their left (Cowan's right) or else fell prone and began firing at the cannoneers. Captain Rorty's four gun battery (just to the left of Cowan's) received most of their attention, and the cannoneers suffered greatly. Among those killed was Captain Rorty. The 1st New York Light Artillery, Battery B was in a desperate situation. Their two senior officers were down, their ammunition was nearly expended, and the crews were too thin to effectively man their guns.[20]

Cowan's battery also suffered from the fire. Among those hit was Private Otis Billings, who had earlier asked to be excused from duty because he was ill. Young Billings was shot and killed as he bravely served his piece.[21]

---

were the case, Cowan would have been forced to withdraw without discharging the canister.

[19] *Bachelder Papers*, 283, 1156; Cowan to Nicholson, 12/19/1910 and 12/5/1913; Cowan, *Herald* account, July, 1911; Cowan to Webb. George Stewart, in his fine account of the third day's battle, believed this statement upset Cowan. Stewart wrote, "The Captain was a little miffed that instead of being congratulated on his determined stand he had been warned against such an elementary mistake as shooting into the men along the wall." (Stewart, *Pickett's Charge,* 223). The following statement was made by Cowan concerning the incident: "General Hunt...was very fearful that my fire would damage our own men, but I was on foot and could see what we were doing better than the general mounted." (Cowan to Webb)

[20] *New York at Gettysburg*, 1277; *O.R.*, Vol. 27, Part I, 480.

[21] Busey, *These Honored Dead*, 173. "Shot in the head..."

Not far from Billings, Lieutenant William H. Johnson fell wounded. Shot in the hip, the lieutenant was carried to the rear. Now Lieutenant William P. Wright was the only officer beside Cowan still with the guns. [22]

After expending nearly all of his canister supply, Captain Cowan gave the order to cease-fire. Desperately short of ammunition, he decided to make the last of it count. The crews were directed to load the pieces with double charges of canister. Once loaded, the guns would remain ready to discharge their deadly rounds if the enemy carried the wall in front of them.[23]

In front of the Federal position, the Confederate attack had temporarily stalled. Seeing the need for a fresh push against the Union line, one of General Pickett's three brigade commanders, Brigadier General Lewis Armistead, placed his hat on his sword and yelled, "Come on, boys, give them the cold steel! Who will follow me?"[24] The forty-six year old general led his brigade toward the Second Corps line.[25]

In one of the true ironies of the war, Armistead was leading an attack against a position defended by one of his closest personal friends, Winfield Scott Hancock.[26] General Armistead led a large group from his brigade over the wall near Cushing's guns. Lieutenant Cushing was dead, and what remained of his battery were driven from their guns.[27] The men of the 71st Pennsylvania were

---

[22] Cowan, *Herald* account, July, 1911; *Auburn A and U*, 7/11/1863, "J.W.C." letter; *New York at Gettysburg*, 1277; Lieutenant Theodore Atkins previously suffered a sunstroke in the intense heat. Information also from Wright's and Atkins' individual service records from the National Archives.

[23] Cowan, *Herald* account, July, 1911; *Bachelder Papers*, 282; *New York at Gettysburg*, 1277.

[24] Stewart, *Pickett's Charge*, 216 - 217.

[25] Mark Boatner, *The Civil War Dictionary,* (New York, 1959,'83); Stewart, *Pickett's Charge*, 29.

[26] Boatner, *Civil War Dictionary*; Tucker, *High Tide at Gettysburg*, 329 – 330.

[27] Brown, *Cushing of Gettysburg*, 251.

also driven back; two companies of men retreated from the wall to join the rest of the regiment, thirty to forty yards to the rear.[28]

Seeing the troops retiring on their right, the men of the 69th Pennsylvania also fell back. The companies in front of Cowan's pieces welcomed the opportunity to move. Facing enemy fire in their front, and at the same time having artillery firing canister over their heads in the rear, was less than a comfortable situation. When Cowan paused to load his cannon with double canister, many of the Pennsylvanians shifted to a position in the trees to their right. For some, however, they took the opportunity to make for the rear. Breaking ranks they dashed for safety, running through the battery.[29]

Captain Cowan later recalled an incident as some of the men ran through his position.

> **A good many of those two Companies of the 69th ran away, Officers among them, as I saw plainly and cursed them...One of them was a Captain. He ran like a turkey, with his sword tucked under his arm, and his face distorted with fear. Corporal Plunkett, near me was raging mad and swore at them like a pirate. I saw him pick up from the ground a dutch coffee pot by the handle and smash it on the head of one of the runaways. The bottom broke in but that fellow went on running with the tin pot down on his ears...I can still see that fellow running away with the coffee pot, down over his ears.[30]**

---

[28] Hartwig, "It Struck Horror to Us All", 97.

[29] *Ibid*; Cowan, *Herald* account, July, 1911; *Bachelder Papers*, 1157; Cowan to Nicholson.

[30] Quoted from Cowan to Spencer, 1/17/1911;Cowan to Nicholson; Cowan to Spencer, 1/17/1911 (again). Also see *New York at Gettysburg*, 1277 and *Bachelder Papers,* 1157.

[31] Cowan to Spencer, 1/17/1911.

The pause in the firing, coupled with seeing some Federal troops heading for the rear, presented the Confederates in front of Cowan's guns with an opportunity to advance. They sprang to their feet and ran toward the wall yelling, "Take the Guns!"[31] Hoping to join Armistead's men in driving through the Federal center, the men dashed toward the 1st Independent as the last of the pieces were being loaded.

Cowan ordered his men to finish loading but to reserve their fire until he gave the signal. The captain hoped to maximize the effects of the blast. This also gave some of the fleeing Union troops time to clear his front.

Corporal James Plunkett, who had been assigned to the battery from a Vermont regiment, picked up some stones and began throwing them at the rebels coming over the wall. William Saltsman joined Plunkett, and the two unarmed men fired the only projectiles they had at the approaching enemy.[32] Cowan continued to wait for the enemy to close.

In order to prevent his battery from being overrun, Captain Cowan instructed his crews to prepare to move the guns to the rear after their final discharge. He hoped the effects of the volley would give them time to pull the guns to a knoll fifty yards behind them.[33] The drivers were ordered to take any of the limbers which could be moved (they had to cut loose their fallen horses) to the knoll and wait. The caisson limbers, which had arrived with the full chests of ammunition from the field near the First Corps headquarters, were also directed to the position.[34]

---

[32] Vaughn letters. Sergeant Vaughn described the incident in two letters home. "…two of our boys stoned them." And later, "William Saltsman, since made Corporal…stoned the rebs. James Plunkett…stoned the rebs."

[33] *New York at Gettysburg*, 1277; Cowan, *Herald* account, July, 1911; Bachelder Papers, 282. The crews probably prepared the prolong ropes at this point.

[34] *Bachelder Papers*, 1156. It is unclear how many (if any) of the limbers were in condition to move to the rear. The effects of the enemy fire had inflicted many casualties on the horses, and there probably was neither time nor manpower to cut the dead and wounded animals free of their harnesses.

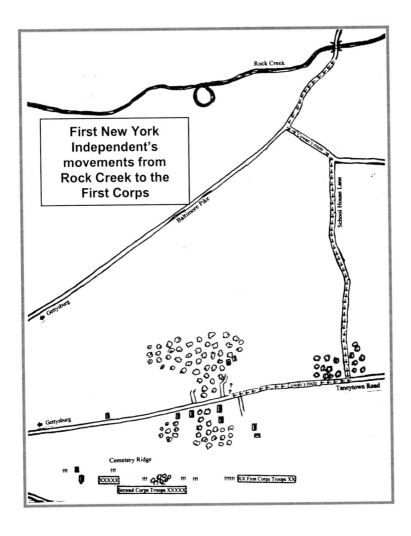

Artillery dispositions along the Secon

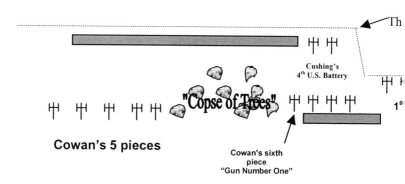

Cushing's
4th U.S. Battery

"Copse of Trees"

Cowan's 5 pieces

Cowan's sixth
piece
"Gun Number One"

**Confederates coming over the wall at the angl
The "High Water Mark" of Pickett's Charge**

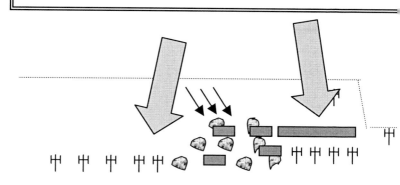

Cowan's 5 pieces

Corps front during "Pickett's Charge"

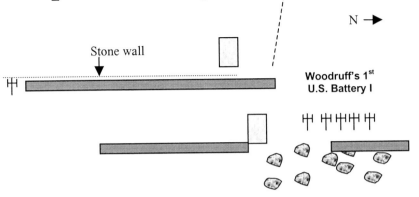

N ➜

Stone wall

Woodruff's 1ˢᵗ
U.S. Battery I

**Brigadier General
Alexander Webb**
New York at Gettysburg

**Major General
Abner Doubleday**
*Miller's Photographic History of
the Civil War*

A photograph of one of Cowan's crews with their piece.

Loading and firing light artillery pieces required a crew of eight men. Four of the men actually serviced the piece, two remained with the limber and handled the ammunition, one transported the ammunition from the limber to the cannon, and one gunner oversaw the sighting and firing. Additionally, the Federals had a chief of piece who was in command of the gun. The following is how Lieutenant Henry Vaughn of Cowan's Battery described the duties of the gun crew.

No. 1...He has the hardest place, which is to ram home the charges. After each firing he sponges out the gun & rams home the cartridge and shell which is put into the muzzle by –

No. 2...His duty is merely to place the charge in the muzzle powder bag first & shell afterwards, & then when No. 1 is tired he alternates with him.

No. 3...He has a thumbstall made of leather and a pricking wire & puts his thumb...over the vent of the gun when No. 1 is wiping out with a sponge so that all fire may be extinguished before the new load is put in...

No. 4...drops into the vent a priming tube which is a tube filled with powder having at the top another tube soldered [sic] at right angles with a rough wire enclosed in percussion powder which is a rough wire pulled out by No. 4 at the command "Fire." To facilitate the pulling out of the wire a lanyard (a small rope) with a hook attached is hooked into the ring made by the end of the rough wire & then [No. 4] standing well outside of the wheel of the cannon, jerks the lanyard briskly pulling the wire out of the percussion, igniting it & setting fire to the powder in the tube which runs down into the cartridge & away goes the shell with a crack & jar that shake the earth under our feet but that's the "music we like."

No. 5...duty of running to the ammunition chest of the gun and bringing the charges as wanted to No 2 who inserts them.

No. 6...His work is to cut out fuses & stick them into the shells & to send fuses & different kinds of ammunition as it may be ordered by the gunner...

No. 7...His duty is to assist No 6 by holding the shells while No 6 prepares them & to alternate with No 5 when he gets tired.

No 8...his duty is to stay with the caisson in the rear & keep the gun ammunition supplied when in action...

The gunner...points and aims the gun at command of "Load," & "Ready," & "Fire."

Cowan later remembered an incident which took place as a driver of the team nearest the trees tried to guide his limber to the rear.

> **...that "wild Irishman" Mike Smith... scrambled on his horse with the confused idea of escaping, when he caught sight of an Irish flag** [carried by the 69th Pennsylvania] **at the right of the trees. Instantly raising himself in the stirrups and waving his whip, with wild excitement, he shouted, "Hurrah for the ould flag."**[35]

Smith's yelling caused Cowan to look to his right. The captain noticed the flag that inspired the Irishman, and also saw Cushings' guns being overrun.[36] With this he turned to Lieutenant William Wright and reiterated the order to drag the pieces to the rear after the final volley. Suddenly Wright fell, shot through the chest by a Confederate at the wall. Another gray clad soldier leveled his sights on Cowan, sending a ball through the "skirt" of his coat but leaving him unharmed.[37]

A young Confederate officer then led a group of soldiers over the wall near the southerly edge of the trees (to the right of Cowan's five guns). He waved his sword yelling, "Take the guns!"[38]

The following is Cowan's own account of the events that followed.

> **Young** [Private Jacob] **McElroy had thrust the canister into the muzzle and fell dead in front**

---

[35] *New York at Gettysburg*, 1280. A similar account is also given in Cowan to Nicholson, 12/5/1913. This action by Smith is depicted in the bronze relief on the unit's monument at Gettysburg.

[36] Cowan to Nicholson, 12/5/1913; *Bachelder Papers*, 282 and 1156.

[37] *New York at Gettysburg*, 1277; Cowan, *Herald* account, July, 1911; "J.W.C." letter, 7/11/1863, *Auburn A and U.*

[38] Cowan, *Herald* account, July, 1911; *New York at Gettysburg*, 1277; Cowan to Nicholson; *Bachelder Papers*, 1156 - 1157.

of the wheel, with three rifle balls in his face. [Charles H.] **Gates rammed the charge home and springing back, fell shot through both legs. Bassenden** [probably George Barrenden] **sprang forward to seize the sponge staff.** [William A.] **Sears pricked the cartridge and was ready to fire at the word. Little "Aleck" McKenzie, the corporal, was running down the sight, to meet the enemy just crossing the demolished stone wall ten yards away, and as he signaled "Fire!" he fell across the trail of the gun, wounded.**[39]

McKenzie's order was apparently in response to Cowan yelling "Fire!" when the Confederates were within tens yards of the guns. The discharge hurled "220 chunks of lead from each of the five guns upon them."[40]

---

[39] *New York at Gettysburg*, 1280. The original account is printed as Bassenden, but it must refer to Barrenden. We know this refers to the gun closest to the trees because of Cowan's description. After chronicling the events surrounding the gun, he then went on to discuss the guns, horses and the "Mike Smith" incident. Before placing the charge in the muzzle, Jake McElroy apparently said, "Captain, this is our last round." See Brown, "Double Canister and the New York Monuments Commission, *In Memoriam,* 66-67.

[40] Cowan, *Herald* account, July, 1911. Cowan stated, "I shouted the order 'Fire!'"

Chapter Eleven

"It Was a Pitiful Spectacle"

> **I saw one officer waving his sword and call-
> ing to his men to "take that gun" just as I
> shouted "fire" – What was the result** [of the
> canister fire] **we did not halt to see, for my guns
> were dragged behind the crest of the hill on
> the instant of firing and the men were drag-
> ging them to the next knoll...**[1]

This is how Andrew Cowan described the events following
the battery's last discharge of canister. As soon as the guns recoiled from the discharge, the men scrambled to their pieces hoping to drag them to safety. Grabbing the prolong ropes and wheels,
they pushed and pulled the guns back to the knoll, where the caisson limbers were waiting. The weary crews then loaded shells
from the full munitions chests into the two serviceable pieces and
opened fire.[2]

---

[1] *Bachelder Papers*, 1156

[2] *Ibid.*, 282 and 1156; Cowan, *Herald* account, July, 1911. "...the two
guns we had in working order..." All six of the battery's caissons were
not at the knoll. Probably only two or possibly three, with the others
remaining in position near Newton's headquarters.

Cowan's gun number one, which earlier had overrun the position and fought from the other side of the trees, did not join the other pieces at the knoll. Sergeant Mullaly received instructions from Cowan to move to the crest after his last round was fired, but Mullaly was soon wounded. Whoever assumed command was probably unaware of these instructions, thus the piece accompanied Cushing's guns (what was left of them) to the rear.[3]

Several nearby Federal regiments counter-attacked the Confederates at the wall. The 19th Massachusetts and 42nd New York rushed in to relieve the remnants of the 69th Pennsylvania, desperately fighting to hold back the rebel surge. These commands were soon joined by a group of First Corps troops led by Colonel Theodore Gates.[4] Gradually the fighting near the copse of trees began to subside and the attack was turned back.

"Pickett's Charge" had failed. The survivors either threw down their weapons or began retreating back across the fields to their own lines. After discharging his second volley from the knoll, Cowan noticed the gray lines retiring.[5] He also noticed some Confederate artillery in position behind them, near the Emmitsburg road. Originally these Southern cannon were supposed to support the attack, but now they were trying to cover the retreat.

Cowan ordered his two serviceable pieces forward. The limbers rolled ahead and the guns were quickly hitched. The able-bodied men then accompanied the cannon to the same position they had occupied during the charge.[6]

---

[3] Cowan to Webb; Cowan to Spencer, 1/17/1911. Some recent historical accounts have this piece as being abandoned, but the following statements by Cowan show this was not the case. 1)) "One of my guns – that to the right of the clump of trees was withdrawn. The sergeant [I gave the orders to was wounded, and the corporal who took command of the piece]...took it back to the caissons behind General Newton's headquarters." (Cowan to Webb)
2) Cowan later described his response to the soldier who had ordered the gun to the rear. "When he came back with it, I was very angry until he told me that he had been ordered to get out of the way & retreated with Cushing's guns." (Cowan to Spencer)

[4] Hartwig, "It Struck Horror to Us All", 99.

[5] *Bachelder Papers*, 282 and 1156.

[6] *Ibid.,* 1156; Cowan to Nicholson; Cowan, *Herald* account, July, 1911.

The guns were again unlimbered and loaded. Sergeant Orasmus Van Etten took command of one gun, while Captain Cowan personally oversaw the operation of the other. Van Etten and Cowan straddled the stocks and aimed the cannon at the Confederate pieces near the Emmitsburg road.[7]

These two cannon soon began firing at the rebel pieces. Captain Cowan removed his coat and continued to service the gun with the crew.[8] Soon one of Van Etten's aimed shots hit its mark, and a limber chest near the Emmitsburg road exploded. After a few more shots another ammunition chest exploded and the enemy guns limbered up and headed for the rear.[9]

After the firing subsided, Cowan walked to the other side of the trees to check on Mullaly's piece. He noticed that some of Cushing's guns were at the wall, but the others had been withdrawn. He assumed Mullaly's gun must have retired with them. While looking for his piece, Cowan noticed Lieutenant Cushing's body lying near his cannon.[10]

With their part in the fighting over, Cowan and his men began to view the carnage around them. The captain walked toward the wall in front of his pieces, where numerous Confederates lay dead and wounded. Among the dead Cowan spotted the brave young Southern officer who had led the charge toward his gun. Beside the body was the man's sword, which he picked up and kept for twenty-four years.[11]

---

[7] *New York at Gettysburg*, 1278; Cowan to Nicholson; *Bachelder Papers*, 1156.

[8] Cowan, *Herald* account, July, 1911;"J.W.C." letter, 7/11/1863, *Auburn A & U.*

[9] *New York at Gettysburg*, 1278; Cowan, *Herald* account, July, 1911; Brockway letters; Cowan to Nicholson. These were not the only Federal cannon firing at the Confederate pieces. After the battle Orasmus Van Ettan was promoted to Second Lieutenant, for "gallant conduct." *Auburn A & U*, 8/7/1863.

[10] Cowan to Nicholson.

[11] *New York at Gettysburg*, 1277. Andrew Cowan later returned the sword to the survivors of Pickett's charge. This apparently was done during a reunion – on the same spot where the young men fell. Cowan to Spencer, 1/17/1911; Cowan to Nicholson.

Cowan was very fortunate – he was the only battery commander near the trees to survive the battle.[12] He was also the only
officer in his battery to escape unharmed.[13] The losses for his unit
were high: five men killed or mortally wounded and five others
seriously wounded. They also lost fourteen horses.[14]

For the survivors there was little time to relax. Three of the
1st New York Independent's guns were unserviceable, and several
of their limbers were temporarily out of commission. The dead
horses had to be cut from their harnesses so that the limbers could
again become usable. Additionally, there were eight damaged
wheels on the guns and limbers that needed to be replaced.[15]

General Hunt and the Second Corps artillery commander,
Captain John Hazard, rode up to Cowan's battery and inquired as
to its condition. Standing in his shirtsleeves and covered with
grime, Captain Cowan informed them as to his situation.[16] While
they were talking, General Webb and Brigadier General Alexander
Hays (the commander of the Third Division of the Second Corps)
joined the officers' discussion. Upon hearing Cowan's predica-
ment, Webb assigned ten men from the 20th Massachusetts to assist in making repairs in the battery.[17]

With the additional help the dead horses were soon cut loose,
and the harnesses removed. The remaining horses were then divided among the limbers.

While Cowan was directing the efforts for repairs, someone
informed him that Captain Rorty was dead. "I saw to it that his

---

[12] Both Lieutenant Cushing and Captain Rorty were killed. All three of
the 1st Independent's lieutenants at the front (Lieutenants Atkins,
Wright and Johnson) were wounded (or injured). Lieutenant Peter Kelly
remained in the rear as he was in charge of the caissons. See Brown,
"Double Canister" and Phisterer, 1561.

[13] *New York at Gettysburg*, 1278; Phisterer, 1560; Busey, *These Honored
Dead*, 173.

[14] *O.R.*, Part One, 690; *New York at Gettysburg*, 1278.

[15] *O.R.*, Vol. 27, Part 1, 690.

[16] Cowan to Nicholson, 12/5/1913. Cowan said, they "found me black
with grime and in my shirtsleeves."

[17] Cowan to Nicholson; Cowan to Spencer, 1/17/1911; Cowan, *Herald*
account, July, 1911; *New York at Gettysburg*, 1278.

body was buried," Cowan remembered, "and I marked the board placed at the head of his grave."[18]

Cowan also instructed his men to bury the young Southern officer who led the charge against their battery. His body was temporarily laid to rest beside Captain Rorty. Above his grave Andrew Cowan placed a board with the following inscription:

A Rebel major,
killed while gallantly leading
the charge near this spot,
July 3, 1863.[19]

Samuel Wilkeson, a correspondent from the New York *Times*, soon arrived and asked Captain Cowan to describe the fighting. The captain agreed, and as the two walked down to the wall Wilkeson explained that he was performing this duty with "a heavy heart." His son was also a battery commander, but had fallen mortally wounded during the first day of fighting at Gettysburg.[20]

Cowan later described the sight which he and Wilkeson witnessed.

On our side of the wall were both the blue and the gray, while beyond the wall the ground was covered with dead and wounded Virginians. It was a pitiful spectacle, and the cries of the badly wounded were agonizing.[21]

---

[18] Cowan to Spencer, 1/17/1911. "That board, bearing his name, [later] enabled his uncle to recover the body..."

[19] *New York at Gettysburg*, 1278. The officer was later identified as Lieutenant P. Fletcher Ford of the 57th Virginia. See Carol Reardon, *Pickett's Charge: In History and Memory* (University of North Carolina Press, 1997), 107.

[20] Cowan to Nicholson, 12/19/1910 and 12/5/1913; *New York at Gettysburg*, 1278; Cowan, *Herald* account, July, 1911. Lieutenant Baynard Wilkeson was in command of Battery G, 4th United States Artillery. The nineteen year-old Wilkeson was wounded when a shell exploded, nearly severing his leg at the knee. He amputated it himself with a pocketknife (that is, he finished what the shell explosion nearly did on its own), and later died. See *Battles and Leaders*, Vol. III, 281.

[21] Cowan, *Herald* account, July, 1911.

Chapter Twelve

Afterward

Dear Mother,

Our Battery has passed through a baptism of blood. We occupied the hottest place, in the center, and our loss was awful. 4 men killed instantly, 6 wounded, and 2 officers wounded...

How I wish I could tell you of the acts of our brave boys, they stood to their pieces when the enemy were 15 yards from the muzzles...[1]

_____

[1]Vaughn letters; also "J.W.C." letter, dated July 4, 1863, *Auburn A and U.*

    List of the Casualties
    Killed:
     Private Otis Billings
     Private James Gray
     Private Henry Hitchcock (mortally wounded)
     Private Jacob McIlroy [or McElroy]
     Private Edward Peto
    Wounded:
     Pvt. Henry Clark, slighlty wounded
     Pvt. Charles Gates, severely wounded (legs)
     Lt. William Johnson, severely wounded (thigh)
     Sgt. Albert Kimbark, slightly wounded (on duty 7/4)
     Cpl. Alexander McKenzie, slightly wounded (leg)
     Thomas Sherman, slightly wounded
     Lt. William Wright, severely wounded (chest)

After the battle of Gettysburg, caring for the wounded became a major problem. Fortunately for the injured men from Cowan's battery, they had been carried back to a small farmhouse on the Taneytown road.[2] Once Captain Cowan was confident that his battery could spare him, he rode to the house to check on his casualties.

He found Lieutenant Wright and Private Gates, both of whom were seriously wounded, resting on the ground near the house. Wright had been shot through the lungs, and was hemorrhaging; his chances for survival were not good. Gates was shot in both legs, with the bones in both limbs being broken.[3]

The men were suffering for lack of water, but the captain had none to offer them. Suddenly he remembered the bottle of wine the woman at Manchester had given him (when he was forced to leave the banquet early). He retrieved the bottle from his saddle-bag and gave it to Wright and Gates. They had their fill and then passed it along to the other wounded.[4]

After making the men as comfortable as possible, Cowan rode back to the battery. The next day he and several of his men came back to check on the wounded. Somehow they then managed to get "possession of a bedroom on the ground floor of a farm house behind the round top," and moved their casualties to this location.[5]

Wright, in the most serious condition, was given the bed. Lieutenant Johnson occupied a cot in the same room. While they were getting the men situated, a Confederate officer whose arm was amputated was set down in the hall. The New Yorkers found another cot and moved the Southern officer into the room with Wright and Johnson.[6]

---

[2] Cowan's "Military day address."

[3] *Ibid;* Gates' left leg was amputated below the knee, and he had little use in the other for the remainder of his life. (Gates' pension records, National Archives).

[4] Cowan's "Military day address."

[5] *Ibid.*

[6] *Ibid.*

Soon after the battle, Captain Cowan sent a telegraph message off to Lieutenant Wright's family. Upon learning of his condition and location, Wright's father and sister traveled south to care for him. Miraculously, William Wright recovered and moved to Florida after the war.[7]

Lieutenant William Johnson also recovered, only to fall mortally wounded fourteen months later in battle near Winchester.[8] Private Gates received an artificial leg, but suffered severely from the wound in his other leg the rest of his life.[9]

Cowan's 1st New York Independent Light Artillery Battery remained in position with the Second Corps until the morning of July 5, 1863.[10] The battery then joined the Sixth Corps in pursuing the Confederates south as they retreated from Gettysburg.[11]

The battery remained in service with the Sixth Corps, and served in the East until the end of the war. They were engaged at the Wilderness, Spotsylvania, North Anna, Cold Harbor, Cedar Creek (where they suffered their heaviest losses), Petersburg and the Appomatox Campaign.[12] It was at Gettysburg, however, that the battery established its reputation and claimed its place in history.

---

[7] Cowan's "Military day address."; *Bachelder Papers*, 1155.

[8] Phisterer, 1561; Cowan's reunion speech, 1886; Johnson's service records, National Archives.

[9] Charles Gates' military and pension records, National Archives.

[10] *O.R.*, Vol. 27, Part I, 691; Cowan to Nicholson, 12/19/1910.

[11] *O.R.*, Vol. 27, Part I, 691.

[12] Phisterer, 1560. During the battle at Cedar Creek the battery had ten men killed or mortally wounded, with another thirteen wounded.

Captain Andrew Cowan (left) and five members of the battery that served at Gettysburg. (From left to right) Cowan, Pvt. Henry Hiser (standing), Lt. William Wright, Lt. William Johnson, and Lt. Theodore Atkins.

Miller's Photographic History of the Civil War

Reunion photograph of Cowan's battery at their monument at Gettysburg.

Photograph courtesy of the Cayuga County Museum

A postwar photograph of Andrew Cowan and his wife with then Governor of Kentucky Augustus E. Willson.

Photograph courtesy of the Case Library at Colgate University

A photograph of Cowan and his men at a Gettysburg reunion.

Photograph courtesy of the Case Library at Colgate University

Appendix One

Andrew Cowan

Andrew Cowan was born in Ayshire, Scotland, on September 29, 1841. He married his childhood sweetheart, Mary Adsit, while on leave in January of 1864.[1]

Just before his wedding he re-enlisted, along with nearly all of the other men in the battery.[2] He served as the 1st New York Light Artillery's commander until he was wounded on September 13, 1864, at a skirmish near Gilbert's Ford on Opequon Creek.[3] He received a brevet for this action.[4]

Soon after recovering from his wounds, he took command of the Sixth Corps artillery outside of Petersburg.[5] He led the artillery brigade for the remainder of the war, and received high praise for his efforts. The following is a letter excerpt from Major General Horatio Wright, the commander of the Sixth Corps during its final campaigns.

---

[1] Cowan to Spencer, 1/3/1910. They were married in Palmyra, New York, in February of 1864. Cowan's military records from the National Archives. Cited hereinafter as Cowan's military records.

[2] *New York at Gettysburg*, 1274.

[3] Cowan's military records. He was shot in the right hip.

[4] *Ibid*.

[5] *New York at Gettysburg*, 1275.

> For your services as a member of my
> staff, commanding the Artillery Brigade of the
> corps during the recent campaign, the last of
> the war, I am under special obligations. The
> artillery was admirably handled throughout,
> and I have never known it more effectively
> used. At Sailor's Creek on the 6th of April, its
> efficiency exceeded anything in my experi-
> ence, and demonstrated what artillery can do
> on the battlefield when well handled.[6]

A few hours after Lee's surrender at Appomattox, on April 9th, Brevet Major Andrew Cowan ordered his old battery, the 1st New York Independent, to fire a thirty-six gun salute in celebration. These discharges turned out to be the last fired by the Army of the Potomac (such celebrations were prohibited and the orders reached Cowan just after the salute). [7]

In June the troops marched down Pennsylvania Avenue in front of President Andrew Johnson. This was the final proud moment for many of the units of the Army of the Potomac. The recently promoted Lieutenant Colonel Andrew Cowan led the Sixth Corps artillery to the reviewing stand, where he dismounted and sat with the president and Major General Wright, watching his batteries pass by.[8]

The 1st New York Independent was sent to Syracuse, New York, where they were mustered out.[9] From here Colonel Cowan went back to Auburn and made arrangements to travel west. In September he and his wife set out for Indianapolis, Indiana, where

---

[6] Letter excerpt reprinted in the "Great Tribute" article which appeared in the Louisville *Courier Journal,* August 4, 1912. Cited hereinafter as Louisville *Courier Journal.*

[7] Naisawald, *Grape and Canister*, 533. "...the last discharges of the field artillery of the Army of the Potomac..."

[8] Louisville *Courier Journal.* As each brigade passed, its commander dismounted and sat with the president while their unit was in review.

[9] Phisterer, 1560.

they lived for almost a year. They then moved to Louisville, Kentucky, where Andrew Cowan would spend the rest of his life.[10]

In the years after the war Andrew Cowan kept in touch with many of his men, frequently traveling to their reunions. He cared for his men, which is evident in his writings and in the fact that he had his military pension given to members of his battery who were physically disabled or who fell on hard times.[11]

At the turn of the century, Lieutenant Colonel Cowan became somewhat of a well-known veteran.[12] Several major newspapers ran articles about Gettysburg and he was often interviewed or even featured. The largest of these was probably the New York *Herald,* which ran a full-page article entitled, "When Cowan's Battery Withstood Pickett's Splendid Charge." He also traveled to reunions at Gettysburg where he was a featured speaker. On one of these trips he was accompanied by the governor of Kentucky.[13]

Andrew Cowan had two sons, Albert Andrew Cowan and Gilbert Sedgwick Cowan (Gilbert's middle name for Andrew's former beloved Sixth Corps commander, General John Sedgwick).

In 1898, Gilbert Cowan graduated from Yale. While attending his son's graduation ceremony, he was introduced at an alumnus gathering as Colonel Cowan. When one of the men (who assumed Cowan attended Yale) asked the colonel "What class?" Cowan replied, "1865. Army of the Potomac. 'cum laudem.'"[14]

Andrew Cowan was married twice. His first wife died in October of 1867, and he remarried Anna Gilbert nine years later. They lived together in Louisville until Andrew died on August 23, 1919, at the age of seventy-eight.[15]

As Andrew Cowan's coffin was carried to Cave Hill Cemetery, it was covered with the Stars and Stripes, but over his heart

---

[10] Cowan's military records; Brown, "Double Canister."

[11] Cowan's military records.

[12] Andrew Cowan was promoted to Brevet Lieutenant Colonel after the war for his fine service record.

[13] New York *Herald* paper, July 2, 1911; photograph of Cowan and the governor of Kentucky.

[14] Louisville *Courier Journal.*

[15] Cowan's military records.

was a folded Sixth Corps artillery banner. This was done in accordance to his will, which contained the phrase, "God save the United States for which I fought through the Civil War."[16]

---

[16] Brown, "Double Canister at Ten Yards," 293.

Appendix Two

Initial Roster

The following is a list of names of **men who initially enlisted** in the battery. Any information and its source are included with the name. **Names in italics** were on the list of names which appeared in the Auburn A & U on July 14, 1862 (just after the Battle of Malvern Hill). **Names with a "g"** indicate those who are believed to have served at Gettysburg.

Names	Age*	G[R]	Brief Comments
Officers:			
Atkins, Theodore	41	g	Second lieutenant, 1/23/62. Discharged 11/21/63.[P]
Cowan, Andrew	21	g	Served as captain until wounded 9/13/64, then promoted major and commanded the Sixth Corps artillery. [P]
Hiser, Edwin P.	38	g	Second lieutenant, 12/29/63.[P]
Johnson, William H.	33	g	First lieutenant 6/21/62 – 11/2/64. Mortally wounded in battle near Winchester, Va., 9/19/64.[P]
Kelly, Peter	23	g	Second lieutenant, 1/7/63. Discharged 7/17/63.[P]
Kennedy, Terrance J.	41		Captain, transferred to 3rd New York artillery 4/30/62.[P]
Kinney, Milton A.	23	gc	Second lieutenant, 1/17/65.[P]
Sears, William[N]	25	g	First lieutenant, 11/3/64.[P] From Cortland County.[V]

Tallman, Lewis C.	18	g	Second lieutenant, 12/19/64.[P]
Van Ettan, Orasmus	27	g	First lieutenant, 1/9/64.[P]
Vaughn, Henry D.	21	g	Second lieutenant, 3/24/64. Killed in action at Cedar Creek, 10/19/64.[P]
Woodruff, James A.	21		Second lieutenant, 11/23/61. Resigned 11/2/62.[P]
Wright, William P.	19	g	First lieutenant, 11/18/61 – 1/6/64.[P]

Enlisted Men:

Aldrich, Benjamin F.	21		Died of Typhoid-Measles.[V]
Ashpol, William	36		
Austin, Willard N.	38		Teamster.[A]
Barnes, William H.	23		Orderly sergeant.[M]
Barrenden, George	19	g	(Probably Bassenden, George.[A])
Bates, Hiram	27	g	
Bissell, Ralph L.	20	g	
Blunt, James	25	gc	
Bodine, Abram	43		
Bradford, George H.	20		Died 11/30/62 of Typhoid.[V]
Brockway, George F.	21	gc	
Broomfield, Hervey S.	27		(Name spelled "Hervey" on [M]) From Sterling, N.Y.[V]
Buckhout, Edward	30	g	From Auburn.[V]
Bumiston, Joajin Q.	18	g?	(Probably Burniston.[A]) "Detailed as nurse" 5/17/63[R]
Burlingham, Truman	21		Died of disease. From Cortland Co.[V]
Burlingham, George	26	g	
Carpenter, Orlando	18		
Chichester, George	18	g	(Probably Chidester.[A])
Clark, Eugene	21	g	Forge wagon, 4/62.[V]
Clark, Henry W.	24	g	
Cleveland, Wm. G.	21	gc	
Cleveland, Erwin	18		
Cleveland, Richard	23	gc	
Cleveland, Levi	21		
Cook, George C.	18		
Coughlin, John	18		
Crandall, George W.	18		
Cross, James J.	27		
Crouch, Jason G.	21	g	
Cuddeback, John	42		
Cummins, George P.	26		
Cunningham, Sidney	21		
Dempsey, William N.	19	g	
Ditton, Thomas[A]		g	(Not on muster roll)
Dove, Thomas	21		Wagoneer.[M]
Dunks, John	22	gc?	

Dunks, Theodore	26	gc[7]	
Edwards, Charles H.	23		
Emerson, St. Clair	19	g	
Evans, Samuel C.	23		
Fowler, Charles H.	21		
Frair, James	18	g	
Freeman, Lewis C.	22		Died of disease.[V]
Funlord, Joseph	18		(Also as Furlon[A] and Furlow.[V]) Forge wagon, 4/62.[V]
Gates, Charles H.	18	gc	From Auburn.[V]
Gaylord, Charles H.	21	gc	
Georgia, Delphi	21	gc	
Goodrich, William H.	19		
Goodyear, Lucius A.	22	gc	
Gray, James A.	19	gc	"Shot in the head" and killed at Gettysburg.[2]
Grant, Robert	24	g	
Harris, George	22		"Deserted at Auburn, N.Y., Nov. 6"[M]
Haskell, John H.	27	g	
Hiser, Henry C.	34	g	
Hitchcock, Harvey	43		Farrier.[M]
Hitchcock, Henry	18	gc	Killed in action at Gettysburg.[2]
Hoyt, Daniel W.	18		
Inman, William	18		
Jackson, John	42		
Johnson, Jonathan E.	26	gc	
Johnson, Reid	23	g	
Keath, Sidney	19	g	(Probably Keate.[A]) Assigned to a bat'y wagon, 4/62.[V]
Killmer, Ira	28		
Kimbark, Albert E.	32	g	Quarter master sergeant.[M]
Kirkpatrick, Charles	21	g	
Lamphire, Hiram	18		
Lamphire, Moses	18		
Lanfare, Leonard	24		
Lawson, John	18		Died of Typhoid during Peninsular Cam.[V]
Lunning, John	18		(Also as Lanning.[A])
Mantle, James	26		
Mason, Aaron M.	21		
McIlroy, Jacob	19	gc	"Shot in the head and killed" at Gettysburg.[2]
McIntosh, James	21		
McGar, Daniel J.	18		
McKensie, Alexander	19	gc	
Meaker, John W.	19		Discharged because of an illness 11/28/62.[V]
Miles, Daniel L.	20		
Miller, William J.	21	g	
Mills, Josial	18	g	
Milroy, William	19		Died of Typhoid 1/15/62. From Albany area.[V]
Mullaly, Peter	24	gc	

Nethbond, David K.	35		Blacksmith.[M] (Also as Nettleton, Davis R.[A])
Neville, James	28	gc	
Newman, George W.	18		
O'Neill, Christopher	28		(Listed as Neill on roll.[A]) Disch. w/disability.[V]
Overacker, Alvah	23		(Also as Alvin.[A]) Died of disease.[V]
Pack, William R.	28		(Possibly Peck) From Jordan.[V]
Parks, Eben	21		Died of disease June 18, 1862.[V]
Parr, Christopher M.	25	g	From Venice.[V]
Peto, Edward	28	gc	Killed by a shell fragment at Gettysburg.[2]
Plunk, Nelson G.	23		(Probably Plank.) From Lewis County. [V]
Reed, George A.	25	gc	Blacksmith.[M]
Richardson, Erastus	29	g	
Robinson, Warren	25		
Runge, Harrison B.	21		
Sears, William A.	21	g	
Seelye, Ambrose	19	g	From Lewis County.[V]
Selover, Morris	21		
Shapley, Charles H.	23	gc	
Shepard, de Esting	23		
Sherman, Thomas	23	g	
Short, John	33	g	Assigned to the forge wagon 4/62.[V]
Slocum, Willis	19	gc?	
Slocum, Albert	18	gc?	
Smith, Charles E.	18	g	
Smith, Glen	21	g	
Smith, Harrison	21	g	
Smith, John	21	g	
Smith, Martin V.B.	22		From Troy, died of disease September 1862.[V]
Smith, Michael	?	gc	(Not on the original roll)
Spencer, William H.	18		
Spore, Henry	34		Died of disease fall of 1862.[V]
Squires, Arthur W.	18	g	Assigned to a battery wagon, April '62.[V]
Stanton, Charles H.	21		
Steele, Henry S.	27		Sergeant.[M]
Steele, John	21	g	Assigned to a battery wagon 4/62.[V]
Stewart, James	30	g	(Also Stuart.[R])
Sturgis, James L.	20		
Taber, Alva S.	18		
Templar, William E.	21		
Terry, Edmund K.	21		Killed in action, at Williamsburg.
Thompson, Nathaniel	26		Sergeant.[M] Became the unit's cook.[V]
Tobin, Patrick	18	g	
Townsend, Eugene	23	g	
Truax, Edgar F.	23		
Truax, Henry F.	18		
Tucker, Henry I.	18		

Vanantwerp, James B.	23		Died of disease.[V]
Vanarsdall, Thomas	19		
Vanderike, John	19	g	(Probably Vanderipe.[A])
Vanduyne, Peter H.	25		
Van Lear, Edward	18		Bugler.[M]
Vine, Thomas E.	22		Wagoneer.[M] Died of disease.[V]
Wallace, Edward	21		Saddler.[M]
Walker, Jerome	31	g	(Also as Walters[A] and Walter.[R])
Webster, William E.	19	g	
Whipple, Emmett	27		
Whipple, Obed	21		
Wilson, Loren M.	36	g	
Wilkins, Henry	23		
Winters, Ithiel C.	28	g	
Wood, James R.	18		Sergeant.[M]

Others Present at Gettysburg:[1]

Atwell, ?	gc	
Billings, Otis C.	gc	Killed iat Gettysburg (22, from Bath, NY).[2]
Brown, ?	gc	
Burnett, Francis (see end note)		From the 5th Vermont
Bushey, ?		
Catline, ?	gc	
Clarkson, ?	gc	
Collier, ?		
Corbett, ?		
Fisher, ?		
Flanders, ?	gc	
Flynn, ?	gc	
Gibbson, ?		
Hendrick, ?	gc	
Hogan, ?		
Housavin, ?	gc	
Kipp, ?	gc	
Martin, ?		
McGinnis, H.	gc	
McGinnis, M.	gc	
Mervou, ?	gc	
Morressy, ?	gc	
Oniddick, ?		
Plunkett, James	gc	From Vermont.[V]
Post, ?	gc	
Reynolds, ?		
Risphur, ?		
Saltsman, William[V]	gc	
Schierby, ?		
Sherwood, ?		

Shill, ?	gc
Sipetrutt, ?	
Smith, A.J.	
Smith, W.H.	
Tharp, ?	
Tighe, ?	gc
Tricker, ?	
Wedge, ?	gc
Wyman, ?	

*Age at enlistment.

A From list in *Auburn A & U*, July 14, 1862.

g Refers to the men believed to have been with the battery at Gettysburg.

gc Refers to the men whom I believe were in combat positions with the guns at Gettysburg.

M Muster roll.

N There were two William Sears on the original roll.

P Phisterer's *New York in the War of the Rebellion*

R Roster taken by Henry Vaughn right before the battle.

V Henry Vaughn letters.

? Vaughn's roster does not specify which Dunk or Slocum.

1 Based on Vaughn's roster. Many of these men probably transferred from other units (Some absorbed from "Wheeler's" battery during the summer of 1862.V)

2 From John Busey's, *These Honored Dead*, 173.

Revised Edition Note:

Special thanks to Cathy Gagnon for forwarding a copy of Francis Burnett's service records (her great-great grandfather). These records show that several men from at least one Vermont regiment (the 5th) were transferred to Cowan's Battery to fill his depleted ranks. This was apparently done through the order of Brigadier General Albion P. Howe, commander of the Second Division of the Sixth Corps. It is quite possible that many of the men at the end of the list were from Vermont units.

Appendix Three

Glossary of Terms

Please note: This is **not** intended to be a manual of
exact definitions, but rather a general tool for those
who are unfamiliar with the terms used in this book.

ammunition chest A wooden box that contained ammunition for the
cannon. Each limber had one chest, and the caissons carried two. A chest
loaded for a 12-pound Napoleon carried thirty-two rounds of ordnance
and weighed about 500 lbs. (twelve solid shot, twelve case shot, four
shells, and four rounds of canister). (See Ripley, *Artillery and Ammunition of the Civil War,* 196).

artillery battalion An organization of Confederate artillery batteries
assigned to divisions or corps reserve. Battalions that served in the Army
of Northern Virginia at Gettysburg are listed below.

  First Corps – contained five artillery battalions, attached to:
   – McLaws' Division – battalion of four batteries (Col. Cabell).
   – Pickett's Division – battalion of four batteries (Maj. Dearing).
   – Hood's Division – battalion of four batteries (Maj. Henry).
   – Artillery Reserve (Corps)
     – Alexander's battalion – battalion of six batteries (Col. Alexander).
     – Washington Artillery – battalion of four batteries (Maj. Eshle-
     man).
  Second Corps – contained five artillery battalions, attached to:
   – Early's Division – battalion of four batteries (Lt. Col. Jones).
   – Johnson's Division – battalion of four batteries (Maj. Latimer).
   – Rodes' Division – battalion of four batteries (Lt. Col. Carter).
   – Artillery Reserve (Colonel Brown).
     – 1st Virginia Battalion – battalion of five batteries (Capt. Dance).
     – Nelson's Battalion – battalion of three batteries (Lt. Col. Nelson).

Third Corps – contained five artillery battalions, attached to:
- Anderson's Division – battalion of three batteries (Maj. Lane).
- Heth's Division – battalion of four batteries (Lt. Col. Garnett).
- Pender's Division – battalion of four batteries (Maj. Poague).
- Artillery Reserve (Colonel Walker).
- McIntosh's Battalion – battalion of four batteries (Maj. McIntosh).
- Pegram's Battalion – battalion of five batteries (Maj. Pehram).
Cavalry Corps – contained two artillery battalions, attached to:
- Stuart Horse Artillery – battalion of six batteries (Maj. Beckham).
- Imboden's Command – battalion of four batteries (Brig. Gen. Imboden).

artillery brigade An organization of Union artillery batteries attached to a corps or assigned to the artillery reserve. Artillery brigades that served in the Army of the Potomac at Gettysburg are listed below.
First Corps – artillery brigade of five batteries (Col. Wainwright).
Second Corps – artillery brigade of five batteries (Capt. Hazard).
Third Corps – artillery brigade of five batteries (Capt. Randolph).
Fifth Corps – artillery brigade of five batteries. (Capt. Martin).
Sixth Corps – artillery brigade of eight batteries. (Col. Tompkins).
Eleventh Corps – artillery brigade of five batteries. (Maj. Osborn).
Twelfth Corps – artillery brigade of four batteries. (Lt. Muhlenberg).
Cavalry Corps
- First Brigade – artillery brigade of five batteries. (Capt. Robertson).
- Second Brigade – artillery brigade of four batteries. (Capt. Tidball).
Artillery Reserve
- First Regular Brigade – four batteries. (Capt. Ransom).
- First Volunteer Brigade – four batteries (Lt. Col. McGilvery).
- Second Volunteer Brigade – four batteries. (Capt. Taft).
- Third Volunteer Brigade – four batteries. (Capt. Huntington).
- Fourth Volunteer Brigade – five batteries. (Capt. Fitzhugh).

battery The basic command unit for artillery pieces. Typically Confederate batteries at Gettysburg contained four guns, while the Federal batteries contained six pieces.

caisson A two wheeled ammunition carrier for the battery. Typically each battery contained one caisson for each artillery piece. Aside from carrying two ammunition chests, there was also a spare wheel attached to the caisson that fit the wheels of the limbers and gun carriages. The caisson was pulled by a team of six horses and was hitched to an artillery limber. (See Hazlett, Olmstead and Parks, *Field Artillery Weapons of the Civil War,* 219).

canister: Ordnance fired by artillery at close range. These tin cans filled with small iron or lead balls were packed in sawdust, and turned the cannon into a giant shotgun. It was the most effective type of ordnance fired by cannon, but could only be used at close range (under 400 yards). (See Naisawald, *Grape and Canister,* 539)

case shot (or Shrapnel) Projectiles fired from a field piece with a powder charge inside that was ignited by a fuse. Ideally it would explode fifty to seventy-five yards out in front of the enemy, and about twenty feet up. The explosion caused marble sized balls to spray into the enemy position. It was primarily an anti-personnel weapon. (See Naisawald, *Grape and Canister,* 539, and Ripley, *Artillery and Ammunition of the Civil War*).

horses A battery required the service of dozens of horses. Field pieces and caissons were attached to limbers, each with a team of six horses (Confederate batteries were often forced into using four-horse teams to pull the artillery, especially later in the war). Additionally, the officers and some of the sergeants (buglers and color bearers) were mounted. Horses or mules might have pulled the forge and supply wagons.

horses – wheel pair The two horses on the limber team closest to the limber.

horses – swing pair The two horses in the middle of the six-horse team.

horses – lead pair The two horses at the front of the team.

limber A two wheeled carriage that carried ammunition for the gun and towed either a cannon or a caisson. It was pulled by a team of six horses and carried three seated crewmembers on the limber chest.

limber chest The ammunition chest on the limber. This chest supplied the individual guns with ordnance during battle.

Napoleon Officially named the "Light 12-pounder gun," it became the most popular smoothbore cannon during the conflict. General George McClellan's chief of artillery even recommended that Napoleons should be made the exclusive smoothbore field piece of the Army of the Potomac. The 12-pounder got its nickname from Prince Charles Louis Napoleon Bonaparte, *the* Napoleon's nephew, because he was the driving force behind its manufacture and use in the French army. (See Hazlett, Olmstead, and Parks, *Field Artillery Weapons of the Civil War*).

ordnance: A typical limber chest for a light artillery piece contained four types of rounds: solid shot, case, exploding shells and canister.

Ordnance rifle (also three-inch rifle) Common rifled cannon used by both armies during the war. It was very reliable and accurate.

prolonge A rope that could be attached to the cannon and the limber, allowing the guns to be towed to the rear slowly while the crews loaded and fired at the enemy.

section Two artillery pieces made up a section.

shells (exploding shells) Fired from a field piece, this thick walled but powder filled projectile was intended to explode in front of an enemy position and break into pieces. There was a major psychological factor associated with this weapon, mainly because of its noise when it exploded. (See Naisawald, *Grape and Canister,* 538).

shot (solid shot) A solid metal projectile fired from a field piece. It did not explode or fragment on impact, but its inertia made it dangerous because it often continued on through ranks of men inflicted heavy casualties .

spacing:
  between each piece (wheel to wheel) – fourteen yards.
  between cannon and lead limber team – six yards.

tools:
  friction primer An ignition device made of two brass tubes at right angles and soldered together. The vertical tube was filled with powder and inserted into the vent of the cannon. When the lanyard was jerked the friction created by the top (horizontal) tube caused the friction powder to ignite. This fire caused the powder inside of the cannon to explode. (See Naisawald, *Grape and Canister,* 549-550).

  handspike A wooden handle that fit into two rings (pointing rings) on the back (trail) of the field piece. The Number Three man would use the trail handspike for leverage when adjusting the cannon according to the Gunners directions, "Trail Right" or "Trail Left." (See Coggins, *Arms and Equipment of the Civil War*, 70).

  lanyard A rope with a hook on the end that attaches to the friction primer. The Number Four jerks the lanyard rope that ignites the friction primer.

  sponge and rammer staff Tool used by the Number One man to first sponge out the barrel (to extinguish any remaining embers from the previous discharge) and then using the rammer, "ram home" the charge (forcing it down the tube to the breech – under the vent tube).

  thumb stall Leather protective cover for the Number Three man's thumb, which he placed over the vent while the piece was being loaded.

  vent pick Tool inserted down the vent tube to prick a hole in the powder bag. This allowed the lower end of the friction primer to contact the powder.

Bibliography

Primary Sources, (contemporary, no later than 1866):
  George Brockway letters, part of the G. House collection.
  J.W.C. letters printed in *the Auburn Advertiser and Union.*
    September 27, 1862 (printed October 4, 1862)
    Early October, (printed October 14, 1862)
    December 19, 1862, (printed January 1, 1863)
    January 25, 1863, (printed January 31, 1863)
    May 6, 1863 (printed May 13, 1863)
    June 24, 1863 (printed June 29, 1863)
    July 4, 1863 (printed July 11, 1863)
    August 13, 1863 (printed August 17, 1863)
  Andrew Cowan letters printed in the *Auburn Advertiser and Union.*
    July 2, 1862 (printed July 9, 1862)
    July 11, 1862 (printed July 17, 1862)
    July 19, 1862 (printed July 25, 1862)
  Andrew Cowan to Colonel John Bachelder.
    Bachelder Papers (and copies at Gettysburg National Military Park
      Library).
    August 26, 1866
  James Decker letter Letter was reprinted in the *Baldwinswville Mes-
    senger* in July of 1963.
    July 4, 1863, to his sister Frances Decker.
  Terance J. Kennedy letters, printed in the *Auburn Advertiser and
Union.*
    January 12, 1862 (printed January 16, 1862)
    January 24, 1862 (printed January 29, 1862)
    January 27, 1862 (printed February 2, 1862)
    April 26, 1862 (printed May 3, 1862)
  Milton A. Kinney letter, printed in the *Auburn Advertiser and Union.*
    September 29, 1862 (printed October 14, 1862)
  "New-Yorker" letter (identified as a member of the battery), printed in
    the *Auburn Advertiser and Union.*
    June 8, 1862 (printed June 20, 1862)

"A Soldier" letters, (identified as a member of the battery), printed in the *Auburn Advertiser and Union*.
 January 11, 1862 (printed January 18, 1862)
 February 14, 1862 (printed February 18, 1862)
 April 21, 1862 (printed April 29, 1862)
Henry Vaughn letter, printed in the *Auburn Advertiser and Union*.
 March 11, 1863 (printed March 20, 1863)
Henry Vaughn Collection, Cayuga County Historian's Office.
 Journal (from when he enlisted in the battery until he was killed in 1864).
 Letters home to his family from the same period).
 Battery attendance log.
"Unanimous" letter, (identified as a member of the battery), printed in the *Auburn Advertiser and Union*. (Note: This is correctly printed as "Unanimous" and not "Anonymous").
 Printed January 24, 1862

Primary Sources, (later accounts and speeches):

Charles H. Banes testimony, *Bachelder Papers*.
 April 24th, 1890.
Andrew Cowan to Colonel John Bachelder.
 Bachelder Papers (and copies at Gettysburg National Military Park Library).
 November 24, 1885
 December 2, 1885
 December 3, 1885
 August 22, 1889
 November 22, 1889
Andrew Cowan's "Military day" address.
 Louisville Courier Journal, July 10, 1913.
Andrew Cowan to Colonel John P. Nicholson.
 Special Collections at Colgate University Library
  December 19, 1910
 Gettysburg National Military Park Library
  July 27, 1913
  December 5, 1913
  December 10, 1913
Andrew Cowan's "New York Day at Gettysburg" address.
Andrew Cowan to General Daniel Sickles, in the Henry Jackson Hunt

Papers, Manuscript Division, Library of Congress.
Andrew Cowan to William H. Spencer, Special Collections at Colgate University.

> January 3, 1910
> January 17, 1911
> March 22, 1911
> May 27, 1911
> June 7, 1911
> December 27,1913

Andrew Cowan to James Tanner, Special Collections at Colgate University.

> July 4, 1912

Andrew Cowan's address at the Twenty-third anniversary of the battle,

> July 3, 1886.

Andrew Cowan to Mrs. Vaughn, originals at the Cayuga Historians office.

> February 2, 1868.
> October 1, 1873.

Andrew Cowan to General Alexander Webb, Alexander Stewart Webb collection, Yale University Library (copy at Gettysburg National Military Park Library).

Andrew Cowan's address at the dedication of the General Alexander Webb Monument at Gettysburg.

Andrew Cowan: "When Cowan's Battery Withstood Pickett's Splendid Charge: Commander of the Famous Artillery Tells How His Men Met and Repulsed the Flower of Lee's Army at the `High Tide at Gettysburg.'" New York *Herald*, July 2, 1911.

Henry J. Hunt letters to John Bachelder. (*Bachelder papers*).

> August 22, 1874.

Henry J. Hunt, "The Third Day at Gettysburg"
Battles and Leaders of the Civil War. Vol. III, 369 - 385.

Articles:

Brown, Kent Masterson "'Double Canister at Ten Yards': Captain Andrew Cowan at Gettysburg'" *The Filson Club History Quarterly*, Vol. 59, No. 3, pp. 293 - 326.

Cowan, Andrew "Repulsing Pickett's Charge – An Eyewitness Account"

Civil War Times Illustrated, Vol. 3, No. 5, August, 1964. (Note: this is an editor's version of what Cowan experienced by assembling several primary source accounts).

Elmore, Thomas L. "The Effects of Artillery Fire on Infantry at Gettysburg"
  Gettysburg Magazine, July 1, 1991.

Hazlett, James C. "The 3-Inch Ordnance Rifle" in *Civil War Times Illustrated,* Vol. VII, Number 8.

Hartwig, D. Scott "It Struck Horror To Us All" *Gettysburg Magazine.* Jan. 1, 1991, Issue Number 4.

Lash, Gary G. "The Philadelphia Brigade at Gettysburg." *Gettysburg Magazine.* July 1, 1992, Issue Number 7.

Naisawald, L. Van Loan *"*Did Union Artillery Make the Difference?" *Gettysburg* (a publication of *Civil War Times Illustrated* in 1963). Reprinted by Eastern Acorn Press.

Pohanka, Brian C. "James McKay Rorty: A Worthy Officer, A Gallant Soldier, An Estimable Man." Manuscript in the Gettysburg National Military Park Library.

Schultz, David and **Richard Rollins.** "Measuring Pickett's Charge" *Gettysburg Magazine,* Issue Number 17.

Sword, Wiley. "Alexander Webb and His Navy Colt Revolver: In the 'Pinch of the Fight' During 'Pickett's Charge' at Gettysburg." *Gettysburg Magazine.* Issue Number 15.

Books:

Alexander, E.P. *Military Memoroirs of a Confederate.* New York: Charles Scribner's Sons, 1912.

Bidwell, Frederick D. *History of the Forty-Ninth New York Volunteers.* Albany: J.B. Lyon Co., 1916.

Boatner, Mark Mayo. *The Civil War Dictionary.* New York: David McKay Company, 1959.

Bandy, Ken and **Florence Freeland**, eds. *The Gettysburg Papers,* Vols. I & II. Dayton, Ohio: Morningside Press, 1986.

Brown, Kent Masterson. *Cushing of Gettysburg: The Story of a Union Artillery Commander*, University Press of   Kentucky, 1993.

Busey, John W., *These Honored Dead: The Union Casualties at Gettysburg.* Hightstown, New Jersey: Longstreet House, 1988.

Busey, John W. and **David G. Martin**, *Regimental Strengths and Losses at Gettysburg.* Hightstown, New Jersey: Longstreet House, 1986.

Carroll, John M. *Custer in the Civil War: His Unfinished Memoirs.* San Rafael, CA: Presidio Press, 1977.

Coddington, Edwin B. The Gettysburg Campaign: A Study in Command. Dayton, Ohio: Morningside Bookshop, 1979.

Coggins, Jack. *Arms and Equipment of the Civil War,* Garden City, New York: Doubleday and Company, Inc., 1962.

Contant, George W. *Path of Blood: The True Story of the 33rd New York Volunteers.* Dover, Delaware, 1997.

Crumb, Herb, ed. *The Eleventh Corps Artillery at Gettysburg: The Papers of Major Thomas Ward Osborn*. Hamilton, New York: Edminston Publishing, Inc., 1991.

Doubleday, Abner. *Chancellorsville and Gettysburg.* New York: Charles Scribner's Sons, 1882.

Downey, Fairfax. *The Guns at Gettysburg.* New York: David McKay Co., 1958.

Esposito, Vincent J., ed. *The West Point Atlas of the American Wars,* 2 vols. New York: Frederick A. Praeger Publishers, 1959.

Faust, Patricia L. *Historical Times Illustrated Encyclopedia of the Civil War*, New York: Harper Collins, 1986.

Furgurson, **Ernest B.** *Chancellorsville 1863.* New York: Alfred A Knopf, 1992.

Fiftieth Anniversary Celebration: New York Veterans, Gettysburg, 1913. Albany, New York: J.B. Lyon Co., 1916.

Fox, William F., ed. *New York at Gettysburg*. 3 vols. Albany, New York, 1900.

Goss, Warren L. *Recollections of a Private: A Story of the Army of the Potomac.* New York: Thomas Crowell & Co., 1890.

Griffith, Paddy. *Battle Tactics of the Civil War.* New Haven: Yale University Press, 1987.

Hall, Henry. *The History of Auburn.* Auburn: Dennis Bro's Co., 1869.

Hazlett, James C., Edwin Olmstead and **M. Hume Parks,** *Field Artillery Weapons of the Civil War.* Newark: University of Delaware Press, 1983.

In Memoriam Alexander Stuart Webb. Albany, New York, J.B. Lyon Co., 1916.

Johnson, Robert U. and **Clarence C. Buel**, eds. *Battles and Leaders of the Civil War*. 4 vols. New York: Century Company, 1884 - 1889. Castle, Secaucus, N.J.

Judd, David W. *The Story of the Thirty-Third N.Y.S. Vols.* Rochester, Benton & Andrews, 1864.

Ladd, David L. and **Audrey J**, eds. *The Bachelder Papers: Gettysburg in Their Own Words*. 3 vols. Dayton, Ohio, Morningside House, Inc., 1994.

Longacre, Edward G. *The Man Behind the Guns: A Biography of General Henry Jackson Hunt, Chief of Artillery, Army of the Potomac,* New York: A.S. Barnes and Company, 1977.

McPherson, James M. *Battle Cry of Freedom.* New York: Oxford University Press, 1988.

Miller, Francis T. ed. *The Photographic History of the Civil War.* 10 vols. New York: The Review of Reviews, 1912.

Murfin, James V. *The Gleam of Bayonets: The Battle of Antietam and the Maryland Campaign of 1862.* New York: Bonanza Books, 1965.

Murray, R.L., *The Redemption of the "Harper's Ferry Cowards": The Story of the 111th and 126th New York State Volunteers at Gettysburg.* Benedum Books: Wolcott, New York, 1994.

Naisawald, L. Van Loan, *Grape and Canister: The Story of the Field Artillery of the Army of the Potomac, 1861 - 1865.* New York: Oxford University Press, 1960.

Nevins, Allan. *The War for the Union: The Improvised War 1861-1862.* New York: Charles Scribner's Sons, 1959.

New York Monuments Commission, In Memoriam, Alexander Stewart Webb, 1835-1911. Albany, New York, 1911.

Pfanz, Harry W. *Gettysburg: Culp's Hill and Cemetery Hill.* Chapel Hill: University of North Carolina Press, 1993.

Phisterer, Frederick, ed., *New York in the War of the Rebellion, 1861 - 1865.* Albany, New York, 1912. 5 vols.

Priest, John M. *Antietam: A Soldiers' Battle.* New York: Oxford University Press, 1989.

 Reardon, Carol, *Pickett's Charge: In History and Memory.* Chapel Hill: University of North Carolina Press, 1997.

Ripley, Warren. *Artillery and Ammunition of the Civil War.* New York: Promontory Press, 1970.

Schultz, David. *"Double Canister at Ten Yards:" The Federal Artillery and the Repulse of Pickett's Charge.* Redondo Beach, Ca.: Rank and File Publications, 1995.

Sears, Stephen W. *Chancellorsville.* Boston: Houghton Mifflin, 1996. Fields, 1983.

_____. *To the Gates of Richmond.* New York: Ticknor & Fields, 1992.

_____. *Landscape Turned Red: The Battle of Antietam.* New York: Ticknor &Fields, 1983.

Stevens, George T. *Three Years in the Sixth Corps,* Albany, New York: S.R. Gray, Publisher, 1866.

Stewart, George R. *Pickett's Charge: A Microhistory of the Final Attack at Gettysburg, July 3, 1863.* Boston: Houghton Mifflin Company, 1959.

Storke, Elliot G. *History of Cayuga County, New York.* Syracuse: D. Mason & Co., 1879.

Tucker, Glenn. *Hancock the Superb.* Indianapolis: Bobbs-Merrill Company, 1960.

_____. *High Tide at Gettysburg.* Indianapolis: Bobbs-Merrill Company, 1958. (Morningside Books reprint).

U.S. War Department. *War of the Rebellion: Official Records of the Union and Confederate Armies.* 128 vols. Washington, D.C.: U.S. Government Printing Office, 1880 - 1901.

Vanderslice, John M. *Gettysburg Then and Now.* New York: W. Dillingham Co., 1899. (Morningside reprint).

Wiley, Bell I. *The Life of Billy Yank: The Common Soldier of the Union.* Baton Rouge: L.S.U. Press, 1952.

Winslow III, Richard E. *General John Sedgwick.* Novato, Ca.: Presidio Press, 1982.

Wise, Jennings Cropper *The Long Arm of Lee (or The History of the Artillery of the Army of Northern Virginia).* Lynchburg, Virginia: J.P. Bell Co., 1915. (University of Nebraska Press reprint).

Military Records at the National Archives:

Theodore Akins, pension records.
Eugene Clark, pension and service records.
Henry Clark, pension and service records.
Andrew Cowan, pension and service records.
Charles Gates, pension and service records.
William H. Johnson, service records.
Albert Kimbark, pension and service records.
Alexander McKenzie, service records.
Edward Peto, service records.
Henry Vaughn, service records.
William P. Wright, pension and service records.

Maps

New York at Gettysburg **maps.** Series of maps which accompany the three volume series.
Bachelder Maps. Reprinted by Morningside.
John Heiser maps which accompany the *Gettysburg Magazine* articles.
Earl McElfresh *Gettysburg Battlefield* maps. McElfresh Map Co.

Index